The Passive Income Myth

How to Create a Stream of Income from Real Estate, Blogging, Stocks and Bonds

Joseph Hogue

About this Book

You've seen the book titles. They start with, "How to," and end with some ridiculous promise of a six-figure income or the word, "from home."

Search for 'How to make passive income' in Google and you're blasted by more than seven million results. You can practically feel the swindlers screaming out at you from the screen.

Making money on your investments is a powerful draw and ripe for all kinds of scams, scoundrels and shysters.

But in the fiction, there's a little truth to be found. The truth that more than a few people have built massive success stories through the four most popular strategies. The truth that many of the strategies can be started in your spare time and require little cash to get started.

This book is about that truth.

The Passive Income Myth is your opportunity to cut through the B.S. and scams to see how money really can be made in four passive income strategies. I have been involved in every strategy described. Knowing what I have picked up over the last twenty years will save you years of time learning and mistakes made.

Each strategy can be read separately or as a part of a complete system to put together true passive income potential.

In this book you'll learn:

- The exact process I used to make more money on blogging that 81% of bloggers in less than a year (page 46)

- 5 simple criteria I use to pick dividend stocks that will create stable cash flow forever (page 88)

- The fixed-income investment that is replacing bonds as the safety and income investment (page 122)

- How to invest in real estate without the tenant headaches or even touching a property (page 30)

- An investment that has nearly doubled the annual return on stocks over the last 20 years, and has another 20 years to go (page 99)

Want to simplify your investing strategy and stop worrying if you'll meet your goals? Check out my four-part Step-by-Step Investing series. You'll get everything you need to lay out a sleep-at-night investing strategy.

PeerFinance101.com is a new kind of personal finance blog where readers share their own stories of personal finance challenges and success. There's no one-size-fits-all solution to meeting your financial goals but you'll find a lot of similarities in others' stories and a lot of ideas that will help you get through your own challenges. Find topics from investing to managing debt as well as retirement planning and frugal living all on PeerFinance101.

Joseph Hogue, CFA

Born and raised in Iowa, Joseph Hogue graduated from Iowa State University after serving in the Marine Corps. He worked in corporate finance and real estate before starting a career in investment analysis. Mr. Hogue has appeared on Bloomberg as an expert in emerging market investing and has led a team of equity analysts for sell-side research. His investment analysis has been featured in advisor newsletters, institutional research reports and in the financial press.

He holds the Chartered Financial Analyst (CFA) designation, the gold standard for ethical and professional conduct in investment management.

The Passive Income Myth

ISBN-13 (eBook) 978-0-9962321-2-8

ISBN-13 (Print) 978-0-9962321-3-5

Contents

What is Passive Income?

Passive income is money you make off an investment without having to do anything after the initial setup.

The idea that you are not actively involved in managing the investment is an important one because there are a lot of scams and schemes out there in passive income clothing.

It doesn't take more than five minutes online to see one of these 'great opportunities'. Much of the time, the only person making passive income is the guy selling his strategy to others.

While true passive income is the Holy Grail for investors, few investments offer income returns with no involvement by the investor.

Sorting through the countless promises and strategies to passive income investment means striking a balance between how much work you're willing to put into the strategy and the income you can expect. Instead of a strict technical definition, we'll be judging investment strategies on a sliding scale for truly passive income. The fact that a popular passive investment strategy isn't completely passive does not mean that it isn't a great opportunity.

While a successful business may eventually deliver passive income as you hire out daily management, we will not include it as one of the strategies. People don't generally start businesses explicitly for the immediate cash flow but more for upside potential in value and future income. For this book, we'll focus more on strategies that can provide an immediate, or very near-term, stream of cash flow on your investment.

How to Use this Book

The myth of making money without having to do anything is a powerful pull. Thousands are sucked into get-rich-quick schemes and passive income strategies every year only to find that the reality is far from what is promised.

The four investment ideas included in this book are the most popular passive income strategies and I have first-hand experience in each. Each has enough passive income potential that late-night infomercials and online blogs have made millions by selling investors on the desire to earn extra cash with very little effort.

I have been actively involved in each of the four strategies and wanted to shed light on the false promises offered by others. The purpose of the book is to help you see through the hype and decide if each strategy is right for your needs as an investor or a businessperson.

We begin each chapter with a discussion of the investment strategy along with how much you can expect to make. We'll talk about risks and how to get started within the strategy.

At the end of each investment strategy, I look at four important characteristics that will help you decide whether to get involved in the investment.

- **Start-up cost** may not be related to the potential for passive income but it will be an important factor for many investors. Relatively low start-up costs are an advantage for some strategies even if their passive income potential isn't as high as others'. Your own budget may limit what you can do in some of the strategies.

- **Time commitment** is the amount of time and involvement typically required during the first year of the investment. While time commitment may decrease after you've built a larger scale, the book will focus on the amount of time required when first starting out. You will need to decide if you have the time and the patience to see some strategies through to a higher level of passive income achieved after years of work.

- **Income momentum** is the idea that income earnings grow faster, once you start making a little money – the pace of cash flow growth increases. Some strategies provide consistent streams of income from a fixed rate of return. Other strategies provide ever increasing income as the strategy develops.

- **Income continuity** is the idea of stability and consistency of income. Truly passive income strategies should provide a stable source of earnings once started, even if your work drops off. This is important for investors looking to use income earnings to pay living expenses or for those hoping to supplement their regular income. You need to decide whether the continuous work required to maintain the stream of income is something to which you can commit.

Armed with this information, without all the hype of false promises, and you'll be able to make a better decision to start each strategy.

The ultimate investment decision will be yours, to your own needs and passion. Having a passion for a specific strategy should be an important factor in your decision. While one particular strategy may require more active involvement than others, a passion for the work will go a long way to a making it a pleasure. Blogs require a good amount of continuous work but if you enjoy writing on a regular basis, the work involved will not seem as much a burden. Conversely, if you don't enjoy being a property owner, then even the relatively lesser amount of work involved in real estate rentals might not be right for you.

The end of the book features a chapter on Choosing your Passive Income Path and some closing remarks on combining the strategies.

I hope this book helps you to make a more informed decision about passive income strategies. I have a love-hate relationship with many of the strategies we'll cover. They can be a lot of fun and offer strong returns but can take a ton of work to get going. Having the facts about the true passive income potential in each will help you avoid being hustled the next time you're offered the sun and stars in an investment scheme.

Real Estate Investing

Few investments have made as many wealthy as real estate. Investment in land and property seems to be the only true constant across the history of investing and wealth building but is passive income from real estate possible?

There are really two ways to invest in real estate, direct purchase of property and investing in real estate assets. Direct purchase involves a larger up-front cost to buy the land or property but gives you direct control. Indirect investment can be made through real estate investment trusts (REITs) and tax liens but you have no control over a specific property.

I began my professional career as a commercial real estate sales agent and still own a portfolio of residential real estate properties. I flipped houses after the collapse of the housing bubble in 2009 and have invested indirectly through real estate stocks.

Real estate is unique among the other passive income investments because it offers the chance to buy a real asset. While you may own the domain to a blog or a certificate in stock, only real estate offers the opportunity to drive up to your building and say, "That is mine." Developing your real estate properties can provide the benefit from pride of ownership as well as the passive income you'll collect.

The benefits of real estate investing, along with the potential for strong returns, are balanced with the fact that it can break you in an instant. The time and cost it takes to develop a real estate business can consume you. People attribute Donald Trump with almost devine powers when it comes to real estate but did you know the comb-over king filed for bankruptcy four times before 2010?

Direct Real Estate Investment

When most people talk about real estate investing, they usually mean either buying to remodel and resale at a higher price (flipping) or buying to rent for a monthly income. While house flipping can be extremely profitable, there's nothing passive about the strategy so we'll stick with real estate rentals.

Like a lot of passive income strategies we will cover, real estate rentals can fall on a pretty wide range of passive income potential depending on your strategy. I know a few investors that simply act as the "money" and do little more than look over reports brought to them by different contractors and developers. Most of these investors started in the business by doing more of the work but have now grown their portfolio to cash flow enough that they can hire the work out.

I started buying houses in 2002, after working as a commercial real estate agent. I bought houses that needed some remodeling work but not a full make-over and then rented them out. I made a lot of mistakes but was lucky enough to be at the front of the housing boom. After learning a lot in the first year, I earned a five-figure income on about 10 hours a week until selling most of my properties in 2006.

The level of passive income you can achieve from an established real estate business is in stark contrast to what you will probably receive when first starting out. The process of finding, leasing and managing your own properties can be a part-time job at the very least.

As someone that has flipped houses as well as managed a group of rental properties, the best advice I can offer is to know yourself and how much time your are willing to spend on the business. A little more money in your pocket every month isn't really worth it if you spend every waking moment miserable from overwork. Learn what you can realistically do yourself and what you want to hire out.

How to get your Passive Income Real Estate Empire off the Ground

There are a lot of moving parts to a passive income real estate business. Before jumping into your first property, there are a few questions you need to ask yourself.

- Do you want to rent commercial or residential properties? I started my professional career as a commercial RE agent before buying my own residential properties. Buying and renting out commercial space like office, industrial and retail will generally yield a lower return but will also involve far fewer headaches. Leases on commercial space can be longer and can contract for the tenant to pay all expenses. The drawback to commercial space is that it costs much more to buy one property.

- In which neighborhoods do you want to buy? I know real estate investors that have done very well buying and renting in lower-income neighborhoods. For me, it was a huge mistake. I fell into the trap of thinking, "I can buy a house for about half the cost as what I would pay in a better neighborhood. Even if I get slightly lower rent, I'm still making a higher return." Wrong! The money you lose on tenant turnover, unpaid rent and repairs far outweighs any benefit to buying property at a discount. I always recommend to investors to never buy a house somewhere they wouldn't want to live. If the business does poorly, you may end up living in one of your homes.

- Do you want to buy fixer-uppers and remodel the property or do you want to buy homes ready to rent? Many investors immediately think that buying a home that needs a complete remodel, at a steep price discount, will yield the biggest profit. This might be true if you're willing and able to do the work yourself or hire it out cheaply. For most, heavy remodeling isn't their strong suit and the home turns into a money trap. I learned how to do electrical work, tiling, and basic carpentry during my first year of real estate but it wasn't easy. I would recommend that new investors start out with homes in need of just cosmetic repairs like painting and carpet to start. If you manage the rental property yourself, you'll eventually learn some of the bigger remodeling tasks and can look to buy properties that need more work.

Your first step into a passive income real estate business, after learning as much as you can about the subject, will be to find your first property and tackling the question of financing.

Financing your Passive Income Real Estate Business

Few real estate investors pay all cash for their properties. One of the biggest benefits to real estate is the ability to buy on borrowed money and write off the interest as a business expense for taxes. Without the leverage of financing, my experience is that the return from real estate investing is not worth the risks or headaches.

While you may not like taking on debt, the loaned money you use for real estate is good debt. It helps you buy an asset that will generate cash beyond the cost of the interest. This is an important distinction from bad debt like credit cards that simply allow you to buy stuff which you want but can't afford right now.

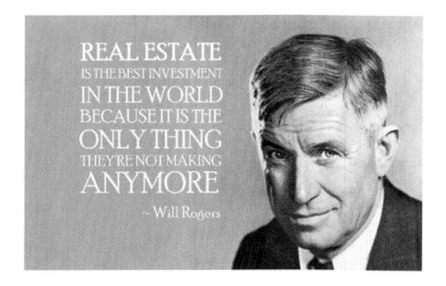

Many new real estate investors take out a conventional mortgage on their first property, using that money to pay between 10% and 30% as a down payment for the new property. Most with good credit scores should be able to get a conventional mortgage though interest rates on rental properties are usually higher than owner-occupied home loans.

Special types of mortgage financing like those sponsored by the Federal Housing Administration (FHA) or the Veterans Administration (VA) may offer lower rates and lower credit standards. These loans are only available on owner-occupied purchases but you can get around that by buying a duplex, triplex, or even four-plex. These small, multi-family properties are usually the best for new investors anyway because they give you multiple properties with the benefit of being more easily managed. Even if you aren't applying for one of the sponsored-type financing options, I would highly recommend a multi-family property as your first purchase.

Other types of sponsored financing to consider:

- 203K Loans are special FHA loans for the purchase of homes that need remodeling work done. The required down-payment is as low as 3.5% but requires payment of monthly private mortgage insurance when you put down less than 20% of the cost.

- HomePath mortgages are available through Fannie Mae for foreclosed homes and can be used for investor, non-owner occupied homes. The financing is only available on foreclosed homes held by Fannie Mae so visit the HomePath site to see if any of the properties are of interest.

Depending on how much equity you have available in your own home, you may be able to refinance or get a home equity line of credit (HELOC) on it to finance your rental real estate purchase. These are usually easier to get because the bank has more confidence that you won't simply walk away from your primary residence.

If you are not able to get a mortgage on the property, there are still a few options available though rates can be fairly high. You might try approaching the seller for owner financing where they sell the property to you on monthly installments. This might not be possible if there's a mortgage on the property since many carry a "due on sale" clause. If you do go this route, make absolutely sure you get a notarized contract with all the details.

Lastly, you may consider bringing in a "money" partner to finance the property. This isn't usually an option for new investors with no experience and no connections but might be something you think about as you build out your real estate holdings. Money partners can lend on a rate basis, a portion of the profits or a combination of the two.

As we'll see in finding your property, patience is key with your real estate financing. If you can wait six months and improve your credit score, you may be able to get a much better rate for your loan. Great deals on real estate come around more often than you think so there is really no need to jump into high-cost financing just to grab a specific property.

Finding Properties for your Passive Income Real Estate Business

There are several places to find properties to build your real estate business. The Multiple Listing Service (MLS), a platform for real estate agents to advertise their listings, is the most widely used. MLS listings are usually on Realtor.com but may be listed on Zillow.com as well. Finding properties on these sites is fairly easy by searching for houses within your preferred neighborhood. You'll also start to notice a few real estate agents that specialize in the area.

You may eventually build enough of a relationship with real estate agents to get good leads. At first, it is going to seem like a waste of time because every agent will have a "steal" to show you. Make sure you are crystal clear about what you want and they'll be more selective about what they show you.

Reach out with a call to several agency offices within your preferred neighborhoods, requesting a brief introduction with one of the agents. Make it clear whether you are interested in fixer-uppers or move-in ready houses because some agents might specialize in a certain condition of house. Getting started means a lot of networking and collecting business cards. Before you go out to see any particular property, make sure you look at it online to make sure you're not wasting your time.

realtor.com®

The banks' real estate owned (REO) pages are often the best sources of value though the loan process may take longer. These are foreclosed homes that the bank now owns and lists on its website. If you can't find the page, call the bank and ask for a listing. Understand that the bank is not in the business of directly owning homes and usually just wants to get rid of these properties. Use this to your advantage and negotiate aggressively to get a better price than what's listed on the bank's website.

Similar to bank REO are sheriff's sale properties. These are usually managed by the county treasurer's office or the sheriff and are properties with some kind of judgement against them, often the foreclosure notice before it goes to bank REO. Call your county sheriff for a list or for the next sale schedule.

While you can get some great deals here, the defaulted owner may still live on the property and could make taking possession difficult. Be sure you know the legal process for eviction and be prepared for clean up and remodeling if you're going to invest in these houses.

Investor interest in sheriff sales has decreased a little since the collapse of the housing bubble in 2009. I went to sheriff sales regularly from 2002 through 2006 and only bought one property because prices are often bid up way too high. Look through the listing of properties and have a maximum bid you're willing to make before you go to the sale. Getting sucked into a bidding war is one of the fastest ways to lose money in real estate, whether at an auction sale or a traditional sale through an agent. Be patient, know how much a property is worth and you will find good deals.

Your best deals, but the most work, will come from properties not formerly listed as for sale. Contacting the owners of abandoned or run-down properties might uncover a deal without the hassle of competition from other investors. If you are looking for major remodel properties, driving around your neighborhood can usually uncover a few potentials. Once you have the address of a property, find your county assessor's page on the internet for ownership information.

Knowing the value of a good deal

Even the worst property can be a good deal for the right price.

The problem is that you need to know how much it's worth to know if the price is right. There are a few ways to value property but the two most widely used are comparable sales and the capitalization rate approaches.

The **comparable sales approach** values a property against similar properties that have sold recently. Write down characteristics of a property including age, square feet of living space, number of bedrooms and baths, neighborhood, as well as features like a garage and central air. You then need a list of all the homes that have sold within the last year in the same neighborhood and with the same features.

If your county assessor is on the ball, this can be a fairly easy process. My home county of Polk in Iowa has an excellent assessor's page with a sales search. You get all the information about a property and can compare it to other properties with a search of recent sales.

The idea is that if other similar homes sold for a certain amount, then your target property should sell for that amount as well. If you are not able to find the search page on your assessor's website, call them up and ask how to get the information. Worst case scenario, you may have to look through paper documents but it should all be public information.

To get a good idea of an average value for your target property, you'll want at least ten sales with which to compare.

Here's how to search:

To get a big enough list of comparables, you may need to set a range on your search. Instead of searching for the exact age or square footage, search for a range of 15 years around the property age and a few hundred feet around the size. If your target property is 1,250 square feet built in 1950, try searching for homes that sold and are between 1,000 and 1,500 square feet built between 1940 and 1960. This will give you a bigger list to compare and not have to rely on one or two sales that maybe were not a good estimate of true value.

As an example, I did a quick search for properties sold within the last six months in district 120 of Polk County. I further limited the search to houses meeting the age and size criteria above.

Notice on the search results that the website already gives me the price per square footage. If this wasn't available then you would just divide the sales value of each by the house's size.

Polk County Assessor
111 Court Avenue #195
Des Moines, IA 50309-0904

Residential Sales Results - Mon Jun 29 14:29:46 2015
33 Records
Date >= 2015-01-01
Living Area Between 1000 and 1500
Year Built Between 1940 and 1960
Des Moines District DM South
Occupancy Single Family

District/Parcel	Street	Nh/Pk	Sale Date	Price	Price/sf	Yr	Area
120-00031-000-000	6008 SW 15TH ST	DM42-B	2015-05-18	$98,500	76.24	1950	1292
120-00196-000-000	6110 SW 12TH ST	DM42-B	2015-06-04	$150,000	.08	1953	
120-01304-002-000	5011 SW 8TH ST	DM44-Z	2015-05-14	$95,000	72.11	1941	
	1405 HIGHVIEW DR	DM34-C		$119,500		1956	
	1306 CARRIE AVE	DM34-A		$76,800		1956	
120-92023-000-000	1414 LELAND AVE	DM42-B		$170,000		1956	
	6807 SW 16TH ST	DM44-Z		$44,000		1950	1018
120-92106-000-000	7004 SW 15TH ST	DM44-Z	2015-01-12	$33,740		1951	1005
120-92121-000-000	7101 SW 15TH ST	DM44-Z	2015-06-12	$111,000	109.92	1951	1067
120-92213-000-000	7304 SW 12TH ST	DM44-Z	2015-05-28	$60,000	42.74	1954	1404
120-92222-000-000	7203 SW 12TH ST	DM44-Z	2015-05-20	$112,000	79.77	1954	1404
120-92244-000-000	7309 SW 15TH ST	DM44-Z	2015-03-17	$125,000	89.03	1954	1404
120-92302-000-000	7304 SW 15TH ST	DM44-Z	2015-03-28	$115,000	85.69	1954	1342

Once you've got a list of similar homes sold within the last year, divide the selling price by the size (square footage) of the home for a price-per-sq.ft value, and find the average of all the properties. Arrange the list by most expensive per square foot to least expensive.

Check out any very high or very low values because they may be throwing off the average. There may be a home that sold very cheaply but only because it needed a lot of work while another home may have sold at a premium on great features. You want to delete these because they don't represent a good average value.

If you are unable to search actual sales through the assessor, you can use properties currently listed for sale on the MLS or through agents. The problem here is that the asking price may not be a true reflection of what the property is really worth. You'll want to be even more skeptical of high- and low-values in this list and I would discount all prices by at least 5% to find market value.

With the average price per square foot of your list, you can make an estimate for the house you are interested in buying. Just multiply the average price per square foot you found by the size of the house.

For example, if the property you want to buy is 1,250 square feet and homes in the area sell for an average of $130 per square foot then the property should sell for something around $162,500 if it is in similar condition.

Keep in mind that this is an approximate market value of the property in a finished condition without the need for repairs.

The capitalization rate approach to valuation is much more straight-forward but may not give you a true market value. It also involves more assumptions than the sales approach. The cap rate is simply the annual net operating income (NOI) of the property divided by the cost or value. Net operating income is the amount left from rents after all expenses are paid but before taxes and interest payments.

CAP RATE = ANNUAL NOI / PROPERTY VALUE

Basically, the cap rate is the investment return on a property. It is the rents collected minus all expenses and divided by the property cost. There are a lot of assumptions you'll have to make like annual expenses, but you'll need to think through these as part of your rental business anyway.

There are two ways to look at the cap rate formula. If you know what kind of return you want to achieve or the average return on similar properties then you can find an approximate value by dividing the NOI by required return (NOI/return rate). This helps determine how much you are willing to pay for a property.

Example: If a property will make $15,000 in annual rent after expenses and you want at least a 7% return, then you would be willing to pay no more than $214,000 for the property.

$$\$15,000 / 0.07 = \$214,285$$

If the seller is asking for much more than that amount, you might be better off finding a different deal.

You can also take the NOI divided by the asking price of the property to see what kind of a return offered on the sale without negotiating a better price. If the property above is being sold for $350,000 then the return would be 4.3 percent.

$$\$15,000 / \$350,000 = 0.0428 = 4.3\%$$

Unless you think you can negotiate a better price, this return is not likely to get on your radar.

Working through potential expenses is a big part of successful real estate investing and we'll cover that more later in the chapter.

Knowing the approximate value of a property is only the first step to getting a good deal. Never be afraid to ask for a lower price and be an aggressive negotiator. The worst thing you can do is rush into a purchase or get bullied and pay too much. Go into the negotiations with a maximum price, a starting offer and several ideas on what you can offer instead of price.

- Your offer will be stronger if you already have financing approved

- If your calculations put the actual value around your offer price or lower, be ready to show your work to prove the point. Be ready with your comparable sales or cap rate calculations to show what the property is actually worth

- Offer to put more money down as "earnest" money on the purchase offer

- Ask for some repairs to be made by the seller as a negotiating point

- Ask for the owner to cover more of the closing costs

Finding Tenants for your Passive Income Real Estate Business

Advertising your rental property can be as simple as a sign in the window. This is actually one of the most effective methods and the one with which I always had the most success. Beyond a sign, online advertising through Craigslist, Rentals.com or other sites can be relatively cheap.

Most of the time, it won't be difficult finding tenants but finding good tenants...that's the trick.

It is so much better to let your property sit vacant for an extra month or two than to rush into an agreement with a bad tenant. You will be tempted to just go with your gut and not check out applicants. Your gut is wrong! Fight the temptation if you want to keep your sanity! A bad tenant will trash your property and cost you thousands in missed rent and eviction costs.

Always run a credit check and a criminal records check on your tenant applicants. You can check an applicant's credit free through Experian and a criminal record checks will cost around $20 through most county court systems.

Good credit and a clean record is not a guarantee of a good tenant but it's a good start. Drive by the applicant's current residence as well and note the car they're driving. If they don't take care of their car or where they live now, it's likely they won't take care of your property.

Again, I can't stress enough that you need to check out a tenant before you agree to a lease. This is from personal experience and mistakes I've learned from with no small amount of pain.

Make sure your tenants understand that the rent is due by a certain day with no exceptions. I recommend using a post office box to avoid tenants coming to your home. Understand how much you can legally charge for a late payment, usually a trivial amount like $15 after a grace period. Explain to new tenants your policy on the eviction process, i.e. when do you start the process when rent is late.

You absolutely must know the eviction process and have a policy for when you begin proceedings. Where I rented homes, you had to send a notice by certified mail and give the tenant seven days. Then you filed in small claims court for an eviction which meant another notice delivered by the sheriff and a court date usually about three weeks out.

This all means extra time and fees. I made it a point to start the eviction process if rent was late by two weeks. This way, I could have a tenant out of the house within a month of lost rent. Their security deposit covered that lost month and all I had to worry about was getting the house back on the market.

It may seem cold-hearted but take no excuses when dealing with tenants. It's either a charity or a business but can't be both. I've seen landlords take excuse after excuse of why the rent isn't paid and wait two or three months before they start eviction. Having a formal process for eviction will keep you from procrastinating and losing money.

Maintenance and Permits for your Real Estate Business

Typically, plumbing and electrical maintenance will cost the most since work is generally restricted to licensed members of the trade unions. If you can do one of these, you'll save a lot of money. I learned how to do a complete rewire of a house within a couple of years and do most of the electrical maintenance.

On the other hand, you may find it easier and very much worth a little extra, to just have a maintenance person handle everything directly with the tenants. Pipes can burst at all hours and managing everything yourself can be extremely difficult if you've got a full-time job. Look for at least one handyman to help out when you don't have the time. You may even want to make a deal with someone to show you the ropes of basic maintenance. Paying someone a little extra so you can shadow them while making repairs is a lot easier than trying to learn from a book or a video.

Your city may require that you have a rental permit and an annual inspection for properties so find this out before you get in the game. This is really where having good properties and good tenants make all the difference. Good tenants that respect the property can make your city permits relatively costless and an easy experience. Bad tenants that trash the place means you'll need to fix everything each year to pass inspection. You'll be replacing window screens, door jams, and every little thing because of tenant neglect.

How much can your passive income real estate business make?

Real estate rentals provide returns through three ways: equity, cash flow and tax benefits. The amount you make from each will change over the years.

Equity is the combination of appreciation and the amount of your mortgage paid off each month. Since property is a real asset, it offers good protection against inflation and property prices generally increase by at least that much every year. In developed economies like the United States, annual property appreciation over long periods is generally not much higher than inflation because economic growth and housing demand do not grow at high rates. Beyond appreciation, you will benefit from rents paying off the principal balance of your mortgage each month. For many markets, you can expect between 3% and 6% return each year from the equity in a property.

The tax benefit to a real estate business can also be a good source of return. The IRS allows you to write off depreciation as an expense every year. This means taking a percentage of the price you paid for the property and reducing his means taking a percentage of the price you paid for the property and reducing our taxable income by that amount.

There are several different ways to calculate depreciation but I always just used the simple straight-line method that allowed for 27.5 years of depreciation. That means, you divide the property cost (not including land) by 27.5 and add that to your expenses every year. Since depreciation doesn't actually involve you losing any cash, your taxes go down but you didn't pay anything.

In the early years when there isn't much cash flow on the property, you might not owe any taxes at all. The downside to taking the tax break is that capital gains will be higher when you sell the property, since your cost basis on the investment is lowered by the amount of depreciation you booked.

Pro Hack: You pay no capital gains taxes on the sale of your primary residence. If you can live in the house for two of the last five years before a sale, you can claim a house as a primary residence and save thousands in taxes.

Cash flow is the monthly amount you have left after all expenses and a set aside for estimated taxes. A lot of investors like to use the net operating income as cash flow but that's not really cash in your pocket. NOI does not include interest on loans or taxes and is a poor measure of how much you are actually making in cash. I've put together a table of cash flow with some basic assumptions that I used when managing my own rentals.

For the expenses that include a percentage estimate, you deduct that percentage of the gross rent. If you charge $1,000 a month then a 10% estimate on vacancy would mean deducting an estimate of $100 each month. A 15% estimate for maintenance would mean deducting $150 each month. This doesn't mean that you'll always pay $150 each month for maintenance but smooths your annual maintenance expense over each month to give you an idea of monthly cash flow.

You may not have all the expenses listed below. This is just a list of common expenses. It is extremely important that you build out an estimate on your own before you purchase a property.

Common Real Estate Rental Expenses

Gross Rent	The amount charged per month
- Vacancy	Varies but estimate 10% a year
Gross Operating Income	
- Operating Expenses	
Utilities	May be tenant- or owner-paid
Maintenance	Varies but estimate 15% a year
Snow Removal	Depends on region and property size
Property Management	If managed, estimate 10% of gross rent
Property Taxes	Varies by jurisdiction
Tenant Marketing	Estimate 2% of gross rent
Insurance	Varies
Legal and Permitting Fees	Varies
Net Operating Income	
- Mortgage Interest	
- Tax Liability	Income tax rate
- principal payment	Subtract since use of cash
Cash Flow	Actual money left over at end of month

You won't see the principal payment deducted on most cash flow calculations. I like to remove it to find the actual cash flow of the property and it's important since we're talking about passive income strategies. Your cash flow may be low or even negative on the property but it might still be a good investment if you are earning a good return through an increase in equity.

I have seen pretty common averages for total return on real estate rentals between 5% and 12% a year for single-family residential rentals with cash flow accounting for up to 6% of the return. Your return will depend on whether you can buy a property at a discount and eventually sell it for market value or more.

Of course, returns can be increased significantly if you manage your properties and do your own maintenance or control vacancy. I have friends that do almost all the work on their portfolio of rentals and make upwards of 18% a year return.

Passive Income Potential: Real Estate Investing

Real estate investing falls somewhere in the middle compared to the other passive income strategies we'll review. The time commitment involved isn't as strenuous as blogging but is much more continuous than income investing. Start up costs are much higher than blogging or online stores but the benefit of loans gives it more leverage than investing in stocks or bonds.

Start-up costs can be prohibitive if you do not have the credit score for a loan or other financing options. Loan standards have loosened since the financial crisis and most can get some type of financing. The use of financing eats into cash flow during the early years but you'll be able to buy more properties without having to pay all cash.

The time commitment for real estate investing isn't as continuous as with blogging but it can be a part-time job if you have enough properties and the wrong tenants. Sacrifice a little return for quality tenants and you'll have less to worry about with repair problems.

Income momentum is good for passive income real estate because you progressively earn more as your mortgages are paid off. As you get closer to paying off the loan, more of the payment goes to principal than interest. Your income will also grow as you become a more efficient manager and acquire more properties. Buying multiple properties in the same area or one large multi-family property will make it easier to manage and cheaper to hire out management.

Continuity of income is also good for real estate investing. Though loss of a tenant or a fire could wipe out your income stream, accidents are insurable and good tenants usually stick around for at least a year. With property, you own a real asset that will always be in demand even when the value of financial assets like stocks and bonds plummet.

Passive Income Potential Scale

Truly Passive Income   **Passive Income Myth**

Real Estate (Rentals)

Overall, direct real estate investing can be a good source of passive income but it can also be a lot of work. As with other passive income strategies, it depends on how much you want to manage yourself and how much you will outsource. Cash flow is fairly weak during the early years of a real estate rental business but can grow significantly with more properties and as mortgages are paid down. Real estate investing also offers tax benefits we don't see in other strategies.

Indirect Real Estate Investment

Direct ownership of real estate is more work than a lot of investors want and the high cost of buying may limit what you can do. Investing in real estate indirectly through stocks or tax liens is a good alternative. These two investments can offer the return of real estate investing without the management and initial cost.

Real Estate Passive Income through Tax Liens

Property tax liens have been a popular real estate passive income strategy for decades. If an owner fails to pay taxes on their property, a hold on the property is placed and eventually sold to an investor by the county tax authority. Sale of a tax lien usually wipes out a mortgage or other debt so investors have the potential to get a property for just the amount owed on property taxes.

Twenty-eight states, the District of Columbia and Puerto Rico allow tax liens to be bought by private investors with more than $6 billion in liens sold every year. The liens work like any other kind of debt. You are entitled to an interest rate on the value of the investment until the debt is paid off. If the debt is not paid off, you have the right to take possession of whatever assets the debt secures – in this case, the real estate.

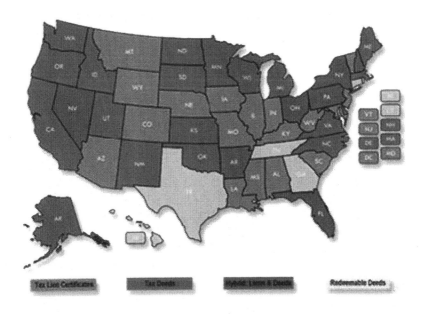

The interest rates on tax liens are usually very high, so high that the strategy becomes the stuff of late-night infomercials and get-rich-quick schemes. In most areas, interest paid on tax liens is between 1% and 3% a month. This means that, for every month you hold a tax lien, the property owner owes you up to an additional 3% on the cost of the lien. The prospect of a passive income investment that pays 36% a year with the potential to get the property draws a lot of investors.

Unfortunately, as we'll see in other passive income strategies, the actual returns and effort involved is usually an entirely different story.

The real story of tax lien investing

I tried tax lien investing in 2003 and can tell you that it is anything but passive income. How the process works varies by county or local tax authority. I will walk through one common process and then highlight some of the other ways.

Almost all jurisdictions hold their tax lien sales through a bidding process, the only difference is how that auction is conducted. In Polk County, I paid $50 (2003) to register for the tax sale. There were hundreds of other investors registered for the sale and upwards of a thousand properties with liens. I researched a lot of the properties through the assessor's page though the bidding process made research mostly a waste of time. Many of the properties were vacant land that really weren't worth much anyway.

In this kind of sale, you are assigned a number for your registration. The auction administrators go down the list of available liens and a registration number is randomly selected. If the investor with that number wants the lien, they can buy it. If not, another registration number is selected. If that second investor doesn't want the lien then anyone in the room can bid on the lien.

- While you're guaranteed that your number will be called sometime during the day, you don't know when or for what property.

- If two investors have already passed on a lien and it goes to auction, what are the odds that it is a good investment?

- A lot of larger investors actually pay people to attend the auction, paying for multiple seats, and then just tell them to buy any property they are offered when their number is called. Most of these are property developers that can work with just about anything they get.

So my experience with the tax lien process in Polk County was a bust. The property that came up when my number was called was a small vacant lot with more than $4,000 in taxes owed. Not only would I have to pay the $4k for the tax lien and any subsequent taxes but then I'd have to do something with a vacant lot if I ended up with the property.

Other counties conduct their auctions in a more traditional bidding process where investors bid on a lien at the lowest rate they will accept. This is a pretty sweat deal for property owners because rates are often bid down extremely low and the property owner doesn't have to worry about paying much in interest. I went to a tax lien auction in Illinois that was like this and the interest rate was often bid down to just under 1% a month.

Yet another auction type is where investors bid up the price they pay for the lien but receive a fixed interest rate. This has the same effect, a lower rate of return on the investment, but the county wins because it gets the extra money.

Call your county treasurer to find out how the bidding process works and when tax liens are sold. Understand how the auction process will affect your return.

If you do go to a tax lien auction, it is a good idea to only bid about half or less of the money you plan on investing over the next year. You will need to continue paying taxes on the properties when they are due or another tax lien might be sold on the property, wiping out your investment. This can get expensive if you get a lien on a large property with high taxes.

The National Tax Lien Association reports that average returns for tax liens are between 4% and 7% with 99% of liens eventually paid by the property owner. While a homeowner might forget to pay your property taxes for a month or two after the deadline, receiving a letter saying the tax lien has been sold to an investor usually results in a check being sent out immediately.

Often, the creditor on any other liens or mortgages will make arrangements to pay off the tax lien. The bank doesn't want to be wiped out on a $100,000 property because the owner didn't pay a couple of grand in taxes.

One of the reasons returns are actually pretty low for tax lien investing is because of this quick payment of liens. If the lien is paid off in a month then you've earned a percent or two but now have to find another investment for your money. Tax lien auctions may only be held once a year so you'll have to sit on the cash until the next auction.

While you can look at assessed value to get an idea of how much a property is worth before you invest in a tax lien, you never have the right to actually inspect the property until (and if) you foreclose.

Still, there is a return available in tax lien investing and it doesn't involve the kind of work that goes into a real estate rental business. If you decide to invest in tax liens, I would suggest researching the process held in nearby counties and talking to a few investors. This will help give you an idea of how much work is involved and what return you can expect.

- Research the counties within reasonable driving distance to find out about auction processes.

- Do your research on the properties through the county assessor page, at least finding how much the property is valued for taxes and how much taxes are each year.

- Understand what kind of a return you are getting depending on how much you pay for a lien. Set a minimum return you will accept to avoid getting carried away and overbidding.

- If you invest in tax liens long enough, you are going to end up getting a property. Have a plan for what you'll do with the real estate before that happens.

- While the average return on tax liens of 4% to 7% seems low, it is not an annualized return. You'll likely earn that return in less than a year to the point where the lien is paid off. This is a respectable return, especially for a limited amount of work, but you need to have a plan for what to do with the money for the rest of the year.

Pro Tip: Map out when tax lien auctions are held in neighboring counties. If you can go to an auction once every two or three months, you'll be able to reinvest your money quickly after your liens are paid. This will significantly increase your annual return and your cash won't be sitting around earning nothing.

Real Estate Passive Income through REITs

Investing in real estate investment trusts (REITs) is the more popular indirect way to get real estate passive income. The concept is pretty simple. REITs are companies that own or finance real estate and issue shares in the stock market against those properties. The companies remove a lot of the barriers that investors face with other forms of real estate investing.

- **Low start-up cost** – Direct investment in real estate means tens of thousands of dollars or more for a down payment. Shares of REITs can be bought like regular stocks for less than one hundred dollars.

- **Diversification** – It's extremely difficult for most investors to buy enough properties, differentiated by location and type, to get safety through diversification. REITs hold hundreds of properties from all over the country or even the world.

- **Management** – Hiring someone to manage a few properties is extremely expensive and you may not have the time to manage your own properties. REITs are managed by experts in real estate with efficiency through hundreds or thousands of properties.

The biggest advantage to REITs is their tax advantages. REITs are structured under a special law that protects them from corporate taxes. If they pay out at least 90% of their annual income to shareholders, they don't have to pay taxes like other companies. That means an extremely efficient way to manage real estate and more money in your pocket as a shareholder. The tax advantage is so powerful that regular companies like

McDonald's and Sears have considered selling their locations into a REIT and then renting the space.

There are primarily two types of REITs, an equity-type and a mortgage-type. Equity REITs own and operate real estate. Mortgage REITs lend money for the purchase of real estate and make money off the interest on the loans. Equity REITs are 90% of the stocks traded and a better investment for real estate passive income so we'll spend the rest of the time focusing on the segment.

Because of the advantages of REITs and the popularity of real estate as an investment, shares of REITs are widely held by pension funds, insurance companies, bank portfolios and by individual investors. With the exception of the recent housing bubble, real estate has historically been an extremely stable investment. Commercial property benefits from the stability of long-term leases and property value that rises by at least the rate of inflation.

The graph below shows the annual returns from price and from income to equity REITs over more than four decades to 2013. Over the period, investors earned an average 8.0% each year in dividends and 5.5% from share price increase.

For reference, that 13.5% total return is nearly twice the 7.2% annual return on stocks in the S&P 500 over the same period.

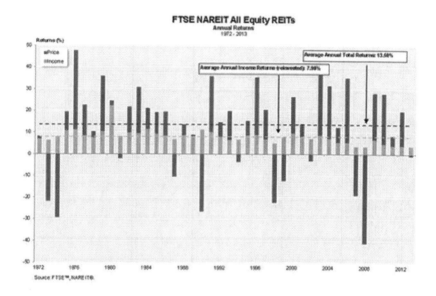

Just like investing in stocks of traditional companies, you can buy shares of individual REIT companies or shares of funds that hold REITs. Even though many REITs offer diversification through properties of varying location and property-type, funds offer one more layer of diversification.

Some good REIT funds to check out include:

Vanguard REIT ETF (NYSE: VNQ) holds shares of 140 REITs in every property type, almost exclusively invested in the United States. The shares pay an annual dividend of 3.76% and have returned 14.8% annually over the last five years.

SPDR Dow Jones Global Real Estate ETF (NYSE: RWO) holds shares of 226 REITs across property types and countries, though U.S. companies still account for 56% of the holdings. The shares pay an annual dividend of 3.0% and have returned 13.6% annually over the last five years. Even against slightly lower returns and higher expenses on the fund, it's important for investors to have some diversification outside of U.S. real estate.

Investing in Individual REITs

Investing in individual REIT companies for real estate passive income is also an option but you will have to make sure you buy enough individual REIT companies to diversify your portfolio across different property types; i.e. industrial, retail, multi-family and office, and by geographic location.

Understand that REITs are different than other companies so they are not valued the same. Since depreciation is a very important part of a real estate business, but is removed from income, the earnings per share (EPS) reported by REITs is not a valid measure of income. Instead of EPS, investors look at the company's Funds from Operations (FFO) or adjusted FFO. The FFO is a more accurate measure of how the REIT is generating cash for shareholders.

The table shows basic calculations for FFO and adjusted FFO. While it can be overwhelming for new investors, it can be intuitive if you think about it. A REIT's true operational performance is the money it makes including the benefit from depreciation but not including one-time things like selling its own properties.

A word of warning, you'll see the calculation for FFO stay pretty consistent though companies and analysts differ on how to calculate adjusted FFO. When you're comparing different companies, just make sure all the calculations methods are the same.

How to Calculate Funds from Operation (FFO) for a REIT

	Net Income
Plus	Depreciation and Amortization from Real Estate
Minus	Interest Income
Minus	Gains or (plus Losses) on Sale of Real Estate
Equals	**Funds from Operations**
Minus	Capital Spending for Maintenance
Minus	Straight-line Rent over Contract
Minus	Non-cash unrealized gains
Equals	**Adjusted FFO**

Once you've got a REIT's FFO or AFFO, you can use it to value the company much like earnings are used for other companies. Dividing the price by FFO will tell you how "expensive" the shares are compared to other REITs. You can also compare the REIT's growth in FFO over the years to make sure they are progressively growing funds.

Analyzing individual REITs can get just as complicated as with other stocks. If you are going to analyze and invest in individual companies, I would suggest putting some money in the ETF funds as well. That will help diversify your investments while still giving you the chance for higher returns on your own analysis.

Risks in Real Estate Passive Income REITs

There are two primary risks with REIT investing, interest rates and property cycles. Both of these are not a problem for long-term investors who will see their investments grow and return cash over decades.

Since REITs pay out most of their cash to shareholders every year, they constantly have to take out loans for growth and operations. Rising interest rates means higher interest expense that might eat into the amount of cash the company can return to shareholders over the next few years. This effect is partially offset by a strengthening economy, usually happening at the same time as interest rate increases, which means stronger rental payments on real estate.

While real estate prices generally go up over time, it's not always a steady upward climb. Prices for commercial real estate, the majority of REIT holdings, are going to rise and fall with the business cycle and the prospect for rent. This means being able to hold your REIT investments without panicking during a recession.

Passive Income Potential: Real Estate Indirect Investing

Indirect investing in real estate results in slightly better passive income potential than direct investment.

Start-up costs are very low for REIT investment with some shares trading for less than $10 each. Costs for tax liens vary quite a bit. You'll have to immediately pay any liens you buy and will need to pay subsequent taxes due later to keep your right to the property until you foreclose or the liens are paid.

The time commitment for investing in REITs can be next to nothing if you just pick one of the diversified funds. Even a little more analysis of individual REITs can be done fairly quickly. The time you spend investing in tax liens could add up depending on how many properties you research and how far the foreclosure process goes for a lien you buy. Even for tax liens, the time commitment is less than direct real estate investment.

Income momentum is good for REIT investing because you can reinvest the dividends into more shares, earning money on your earnings. For tax lien investing, income momentum is not as good because the rate you earn is fixed when you buy the lien. You can reinvest the money you earn but it might be at a lower rate and you'll have to wait for the next lien auction.

Continuity of income is generally good for REIT investing. Most of these companies are very large and cash flows are stable. With REITs, there's possibility that tax law changes will remove the advantages they enjoy which would cause stock prices to crash. This isn't likely to happen because of the affect it would have on real estate prices and the range of investors that count on REIT income.

Income continuity is poor for tax lien investing because you really don't know when the lien will be paid off. Once the lien is paid, your stream of income halts. Even if you have several liens, the potential for all of them to pay off within a few months is high. This can be mitigated by investing in liens across different counties with different auction schedules.

Passive Income Potential Scale

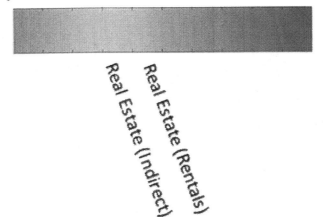

Truly Passive Income   Passive Income Myth

Real Estate (Indirect)
Real Estate (Rentals)

Overall, indirect real estate investing through REITs can be a great source of passive income though returns may not be as high as with direct real estate investing. Investing through tax liens offers better passive income potential than direct management of real estate but not as good as with REITs.

Blogging and Online Stores

One of the biggest passive income myths is that of making money online. Follow the promises of some blogs, mainly those offering blogging services or "how-to" manuals, and you need only register your website name and wait for checks to deposit into your bank account. While blogging can offer some passive income potential, it is much more a traditional job than a passive income investment.

I like to make the analogy that making money online is a lot like real estate investment in raw land. If you buy a piece of land, it may take years to develop it into a profitable commercial or residential space. You may see little income over those years, and certainly not passive income. If you have the patience and the drive for the investment, it can offer the pride of development as well as a strong income.

Developing online assets is similar. You take an undeveloped spot on the internet and build it into a valuable asset, usually with almost no cash flow until you do. As someone that owns two blogs and has contributed to others for more than five years, I know the work that goes into developing an online asset and the income you can expect.

We will cover blogging and running an online store separately in the book. I have seen both created and managed separately but in truth, they work much better combined as one income strategy.

Blogging for passive income

Web firm Technorati found in a 2008 survey that only 7.4 million of the 133 million blogs online had been updated within the previous 120 days. That means 95% of bloggers had quit and abandoned their dream within about four months.

There's a reason for the high rate of blogger burnout.

A survey of bloggers in 2008 by Problogger.net found that 37% of blogs make no money at all. Of those that make money from their blog, 70% said they made less than $500 per month.

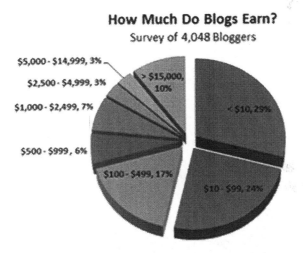

How Much Do Blogs Earn?
Survey of 4,048 Bloggers

$5,000 - $14,999, 3%
$2,500 - $4,999, 3%
$1,000 - $2,499, 7%
$500 - $999, 6%
$100 - $499, 17%
> $15,000, 10%
< $10, 29%
$10 - $99, 24%

Source: Problogger.net (data)

Granted, there are probably many that blog simply as a way to share their thoughts and really don't attempt to make any money. The pie chart includes only those bloggers that have tried to make money blogging but paints a fairly dismal picture of the myth of becoming the next internet millionaire through an online property.

But the fact that 13% of bloggers reported making more than $5,000 a month shows that it is possible to make a good living.

In fact, I make just over $700 a month on my two blogs. That's better than 81% of bloggers, including those that make no money at all, and my two blogs have been live for less than a year. Building a profitable blog takes work but the process I'll share later in the chapter does work.

Blogs make money primarily through four methods:

- Advertising

- Sponsored Posts

- Affiliate Advertising

- Selling Own Products or Services

We'll cover advertising and sponsored posts in this chapter and leave affiliate ads and product sales for the next chapter, online stores, though they can also be sold through a blog.

Blogs make money through advertising by selling space on the site, usually through boxes of text or picture ads. Most bloggers do this through a distributor like Google Adsense which contracts with advertisers to pay a certain amount every time someone clicks on their ad (cost per click, CPC). Google then uses a computer program to place ads on your blog that are relevant to your readers, based on what you talk about in the blog and what they search for on the internet.

Remember: The Adsense ads you see on your blog may not be the ones other see. The computer program shows different ads depending on what people look at on the internet.

If a reader clicks on an ad, Google charges the advertiser and gives you a percentage of the payment. Most advertising works this way, through per-click payments, while other ads pay depending on how many thousand times they show up on your blog (cost per mille, CPM).

Once your blog is large enough, advertisers will pay you to write about their product or simply sponsor you to write about something related to their product. These sponsored posts offer a flat fee, usually starting around $100 and up, to include a mention of the advertiser and a link back to their website. Readers do not have to click on the link or buy anything for the blogger to get paid.

Why Blogging is NOT Passive Income

Of all the passive income ideas we'll cover in this book, blogging is probably the least passive. Take it from someone that manages two blogs, running a site is at least a part-time job and can consume your life. Even in your "free-time" you'll worry over your blog and how to increase traffic.

As the survey above showed, most blogs make little or no money. The blogs that make money are usually more than a few years old. In fact, most blogs see very little traffic over the first few months. The screenshot below is data from a blogger friend of mine that started February 2011. Her blog attracted barely 1,000 readers a month for several months before she was able to get some strong publicity in her sixth month of blogging. It wasn't until after the ninth month that she was consistently getting more than 10,000 visitors a month.

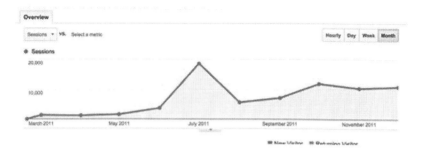

While 10,000 visitors may seem like a profitable website, it will likely earn less than $500 per month. While you'll get paid per clicks for advertising, most sites get around $1 per click and the average varies by type of website.

The average click-through-rate (CTR), or the number of people that click an ad per every 100 page views is less than one percent. If those 10,000 visitors viewed an average of 1.5 pages each then those 15,000 page views might translate to $150 a month from advertising (15,000 times 0.01 click-through rate times $1 per click).

How Blogs Make Money
How 10,000 monthly visitors become $150 a month

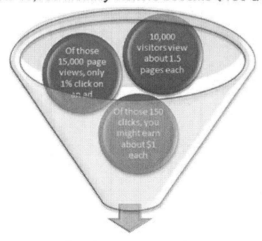

10,000 visitors view about 1.5 pages each

Of those 15,000 page views, only 1% click on an ad

Of those 150 clicks, you might earn about $1 each

$150 a month

Add in another $300 from sponsored posts and affiliate ads (more on this later) and you might make $450 a month for a similar blog.

Now consider the amount of work that goes into a blog over that first year. You need to be posting at least twice a week to build an audience and your place in search rankings. If you are not a strong writer, you'll likely spend at least four hours or more on each post. There is a blogger saying that goes, "Spend two hours promoting your posts for every hour you spend writing."

While social media makes it pretty easy to share and I wouldn't say you need to spend quite that much time promoting your blog, you will spend considerable time commenting, guest blogging and sharing.

Over the first six months of blogging, you will likely have spent a minimum of 500 hours setting up, writing and promoting the blog. For this, you will be lucky to have made a couple hundred dollars through advertising. New blogs will not see much money from sponsored posts or other methods because they don't have enough visitors.

Do the math (a few hundred dollars divided by 500 hours equals the kind of hourly wage even Nike would be ashamed of), and you can see why most bloggers quit before their site reaches six months old.

So Why do People Blog if Passive Income is a Myth?

Now that I have scared most of you, you're probably wondering why anyone bothers blogging at all. Why did bloggers create more than 56 million blog posts in the month of April 2015 on WordPress alone?

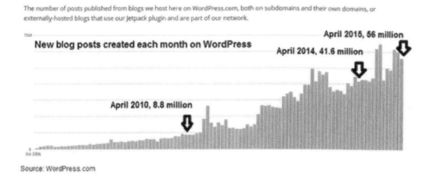

Source: WordPress.com

Because blogging can make you money. Remember the Problogger survey at the beginning of the chapter and the small percentage making five-figures a month? Besides the promise of income, blogging brings with it other benefits and can be done by nearly everybody at very little cost.

A lot of bloggers enjoy the fact that their message is read by thousands, even hundreds of thousands of people every month. They are passionate about their blog and the community they build. This is enough to keep a lot of people blogging without even the thought of making any money.

While blogging may not be entirely passive income, it can build to big money and a semi-passive stream of income. I say semi-passive because you will always need to continue posting to your blog and communicating with readers to keep the income stream from dying off.

Once you build a highly-trafficked blog, it will continue to bring visitors and make money but it will always require at least some upkeep. That's why I say that blogging is the biggest passive income myth, because it is more like a business than a hands-off investment that generates income without constant activity.

Starting your Successful Blog for...Semi-Passive Income

If you have the patience and passion to develop your own web property, the payoff can be pretty remarkable. While there is no one process for creating a successful blog, the process below helped me to earn more than four-fifths of bloggers in less than a year.

Your first job in creating a blog is to pick a **domain name**, which is the name of your website.

- Stick with the standard .com name unless you run a charitable organization, in which case .org works just as well.

- Check out a search site like Instant Domain Search to make sure your site name is available or to get ideas on a name.

- If your "perfect" domain name is taken, try adding things like "a," "the," or "my," but generally avoid hyphens.

- Simple and easy to remember is the key. Take your time because it is very difficult to change your domain once you've already got things running.

Next you will need to choose a web host for your site which will store your site on its servers and provide support. I have used GoDaddy with another site but was not happy with the features provided and switched to BlueHost.

Once you've signed up for hosting you will need to install WordPress onto your site. WordPress is the site builder you will use and where you will manage all the behind-the-scenes stuff for your site.

The process to install WordPress is pretty easy. You'll enter your domain name and create login information. When the installation is complete, click "View Credentials" to see the website address where you will access WordPress for your blog.

This URL address for your blog, will look something like: http://www.yourblogname.com/wp-admin.

After you login to WordPress is when the real fun begins. Within Wordpress is where you will start to build your blog. Along the left-hand side of the screen you will see your menu.

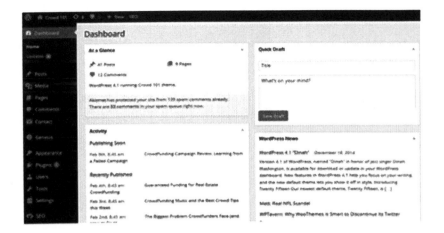

You first need to set up your blog details under the "Settings" item. Fill out your site name, a catchy tagline, and your contact email. Under the settings menu, you will see other sub-menu items. The great thing about WordPress is that a lot of the background stuff is already filled out and you really only need to change a few things.

- For permalinks, use the standard post title without dates. This will be important later for republishing old posts.

- Check out all the sub-headings just to get a feel for where things are in case you want to change something in the future.

The look of your blog is called a Theme, and you can find different ones under the "Appearance" menu item. WordPress offers several options for free and most people will be fine with one of these.

Once you've got a theme installed, your blog is starting to take shape. You now need pages which are just main screens for your site. Almost everyone will need a few basic pages like About Me, Contact and your main Blog page. Beyond that, you might want other pages that are important to your site or a product page to post your store.

Creating a page is just a matter of clicking on the "Pages" menu item then "Add New." You will give your page a name, add content and images, and fill out some SEO information which we will talk about later.

Once all your pages are constructed, you will want to set up your menu which is under the "Appearance" item. Most sites have a Main Menu across the top of their website and a Footer menu that is down at the very bottom. Main menus help people get around while footer menus relay other valuable information like disclaimers and contact info. Place the pages in your menu in the order you want though the About Me page is usually the first on the left.

Next, you'll add plugins to your blog. These are really cool tools that people have created to help you do things without needing to know computer programming. Clicking on "Add New" after "Plugins" will bring up a screen where you can search and select plugins.

Note: Some plugins are free while you'll have to pay for others. I use a few premium plugins but you can build a really great blog on just free ones as well. When looking at new plugins, make sure you look at the most recent update and how many people have downloaded it. Plugins that no one uses might not be updated very often and might stop working.

The plugins I use on my site are:

- Akismet—It comes preloaded on your site and is a great way to protect from spammers in your blog comments. The plugin automatically screens comments and will notify you when a legitimate comment needs approved.

- Broken Link Checker—Nothing is more annoying than clicking on a link in a website and getting a dead end. This plugin monitors all the links on your website and notifies you if one of them is not working.

- Digg Digg— This is the floating (moving) social share buttons you see on the left-side of the screen. Really a cool way to get people to share your posts.

- EWWW Image Optimizer—Images can slow down the time it takes for your website to load on the computer, which is hugely annoying for visitors. An image optimizer plugin helps to reduce the image file sizes without changing how they look.

- OptinSkin—This is a paid plugin but offers a nice tool to make pop-ups and subscriber forms. Not an absolute necessity but worth the money since you only need to buy it once and you can use it on as many websites as you want.

- WordPress Popular Posts—This plugin displays the most popular posts and is customizable for where you want it to show and which posts to show.

- WordPress SEO by Yoast—This is one of the most popular plugins and really helps keep track of your search engine optimization, which we'll get to later.

- WP Super Cache—This is another one that helps improve your site loading speed.

Most plugins are easy to install and come pre-loaded with the most common settings. Once you've got your plugins installed, you will want to finalize how your site looks by managing widgets. Widgets are just tools that let you place a plugin or item in a certain place on your blog. Go to "Appearance" and then to "Widgets."

Moving these widgets around and customizing them is also pretty easy. You will place them in different spots of your website. The widgets are shown on the left half of the screen and you have website areas on the right side. You just drag a widget to that area and it will show up as a dropdown item (i.e., the Text widget in my Header Right section). By clicking on the dropdown for the widget, you can customize how it shows up on the site.

I like to include WordPress Popular Posts and a User Profile at the top of the Primary Sidebar (the right-hand column of the site). That showcases some of your best work for visitors and introduces yourself.

Once your blog is all set up, you will want to start writing. Click on "Posts" and "Add New." – this is where the 'blogging' of owning a blog comes in.

You'll first add the title and the content for the post. I write all my posts up in Microsoft Word and store them in a file for easy organization and then paste it right into WordPress. You can also just type it right into WordPress as well.

Linking to your other posts helps to keep people reading and helps improve your ranking in Google by telling the search engine that this post is important. Linking to other sites is a helpful way to share information and build relationships with other bloggers.

To link words from your content to another website or to another post in your website, highlight the words and click on the little chain symbol in the tool bar. Input the website address to where you want to link and check the "Open in New Window" box so people clicking the link do not get taken away from your site.

A note on post length, the standard thinking is that search engines will not look at your post unless it is more than 300 words long. This is misleading and leads to a lot of bloggers pumping out poor quality posts between 400 and 600 words long. Getting found by the search engines is about quality, not quantity. In fact, research on the length of top ten posts that appear in search shows that average length is around 2,000 words.

There are a couple of reasons why this happens. First, if you are writing about a specific topic and you cover four pages of material then the post is likely to include a lot of keywords that will be picked up by Google. The other reason is that super-size posts, quality ones anyway, are more likely to have information that is useful to readers. That makes the post more likely to be shared which is a big factor for the search engines. If Google sees that a post is shared hundreds of times then it assumes it must be quality content and puts it higher in search rankings.

Adding images into your posts is a good way to break up the monotony of reading a long article. Put the cursor where you want the image to show and click "Add Media." You will either add the image from your library or upload it from your computer. Make sure you include a title, caption and description for the image. The search engines scan images also and it is a way to help your search ranking when someone looks for a keyword.

You will want to add categories to your blog and place your posts in one or more. This helps visitors go directly to material that interests them most.

An important part of your post is the Featured Image, selected at the lower-right corner in WordPress. This is the image that will show on your blog page before people click through to your article. A really interesting image can help persuade people to click through and read the post. As with other images, it is important to add meta information and descriptions so the search engines know what the image is about and can help you get found.

If you installed WordPress SEO by Yoast, making your post search engine friendly is really easy. Search engine optimization (SEO) is a set of tasks that makes your site or individual posts stand out to the search engines like Google and Bing. The more you stand out, the higher up in search you'll appear and the more people will click to your site.

The first part of SEO is picking a keyword that is relevant to the post. A lot of bloggers spend a ton of time picking keywords but I am not really sure it's necessary. Your keyword is the main topic or idea for your post. Your keyword should be natural to the material and should be pretty easy to pick out after you've written the post. For good keyword optimization:

- Try to have it in the title if it sounds natural

- Include it somewhere in the first and last paragraphs

- Include your keyword in headings throughout the post

- The "Meta Description" is what will show up to describe the post in search results. It is a one- or two-sentence teaser description and should include the keyword

As mentioned, a lot of people spend tons of time on keywords. They stuff it into the post until reading becomes awkward. They increase the font size of the keyword to the point that it looks ridiculous. These things used to be old tricks to "fool" the search engines but really don't work much anymore. Just write good articles that will interest readers and the search engines will find you.

You can either publish the post immediately by clicking "Publish" or you can schedule it to automatically publish later by clicking "Edit." I write up all my posts at least a few days ahead of schedule and then just load them up. This helps to make sure that you publish new posts regularly even if something comes up at the last minute. Readers appreciate some regularity for a blog and keeping to some kind of a schedule will be rewarded by constant readership.

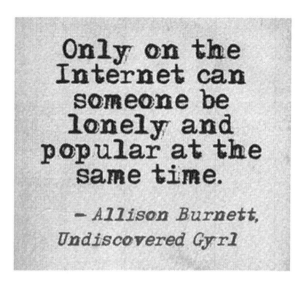

Only on the Internet can someone be lonely and popular at the same time.

— Allison Burnett,
Undiscovered Gyrl

Blogging Rules to Live By

If you have ever made writing a profession and had to answer to an editor, you will love blogging for the freedom you have over your own material. You still need to proof your posts and make sure it's quality content but you won't have to answer to some kid fresh out of college citing his own personal writing style. That said, there are still some rules you need to follow within the blogoverse.

- **Don't steal!** Copying a post from another website will be discovered. There are plugins that will notify a website if their material is being copied and search engines will punish your website.

- **Don't libel or print false information about someone.** This could open up legal problems and why do you need to bad-mouth someone anyway?

- **Understand fair use of images.** Never use a picture that is copyrighted or that you do not have the right to use. If you are looking for images to use for posts, make sure you are searching within Google for "creative commons," which means that they can be used without permission.

Posting to your Blog to Make Money

Once you've got your blog set up, it's time to start putting your thoughts out there and getting people to visit. How often you should contribute to your blog is a popular question among new bloggers. Each new blog post is an opportunity to get a new reader and an opportunity for Google to display your blog in its search results. You want to balance this opportunity with the time and patience you have for blogging. I see a lot of new bloggers start out posting four times a week or even everyday. Most get frustrated and burn out pretty quickly and neglect their site altogether.

If you are maintaining a full-time job while starting your blog, I would recommend two blog posts a week. This will give your readers a stream of fresh content but will help avoid burn out on your part. Some bloggers might disagree with me, but posting more than two or three days a week is not going to help a great deal in the beginning anyway. A big part of how Google ranks posts to display in search is based on a website's age, meaning you can be posting stellar content frequently and you still won't show up on that fabled first-page if your blog is less than a year old.

The best advice I can offer for your new blog is to spend very little time worrying about SEO and blog development in the first three months. Write two or three times a week about things that come naturally to the topic and that are top-of-mind. Spend about as much time reaching out to the community of bloggers in your topic and promoting your posts as you do writing. Spend only as much time on the blog as you are comfortable without sacrificing time with your family and friends.

All this will help you avoid burnout and make the blog more of an enjoyable hobby than work for which you NEED to get paid. It makes seeing those super-small checks for your efforts easier to stomach and you'll stick through it to see bigger paydays.

Making Money from Your Blog

Let's go into more detail about how to make money from your blog and what you can expect from each source. The secret to making money on a blog is to make money through multiple streams of revenue, i.e. through advertising, sponsored posts, affiliates and your own products. Few single sources will make much money alone, unless you've got a stellar product or service to promote. We'll cover advertising and sponsored posts here and hit on affiliate ads and your own products in the next chapter.

Selling advertising space on a blog generally accounts for most of a blogger's income. I have seen estimates from 50% to as high as 80% of a blog's income from advertising.

It's fairly simple to set up a Google Adsense account and you can link multiple blogs to one account. Once everything is verified, you can start placing ads on your blog. I recommend downloading the official Google Adsense Plugin on your blog which makes it very easy to place your ad boxes.

Adsense allows you to position up to three advertising boxes on each page, along with up to three "Link Unit" ads which are simple boxes with text links. There is no rule that says you MUST max out your advertising on a page. Overwhelming your readers with advertising can limit how many return in the future. I've seen a lot of sites restrict their advertising to two boxes per page along with a couple of link unit ads.

There are two important ideas to remember when placing advertising on your blog. First, advertising does no good if people do not see it. Place at least one advertising box so that it will appear without the reader having to scroll down. This is called, "above the fold."

The second idea when determining where to put your ads follows where people look when they visit a website. Google and other advertisers have spent a lot of money tracking reader's attention when they visit a site. The result is the heat map below with red areas getting the most attention, followed by orange and then lighter shades.

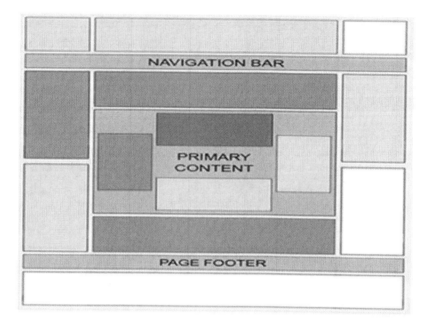

It should be obvious that readers' attention would be focused within the area where content usually goes. You should always include at least one advertising box above, below or within your article. For layouts that include a sidebar on the left side of the screen, this is usually an effective ad spot as well because people read from left-to-right.

Because the right sidebar has traditionally carried advertising, readers have learned to subconsciously ignore a lot of the material on the right side. It can still be a good space for advertising, especially for above-the-fold ads but will probably not be your best placement.

Adsense will do a lot of stuff for you if you allow it. The program will automatically choose the size of the advertising box to maximize revenue and will try to place ads that are more relevant to your audience. You can adjust these features but most bloggers just let the program do the work. On my own blogs, I have adjusted a few of the sidebar ads to display in

300x250 boxes rather than larger boxes. The smaller box, compared to a 300x600 sidebar box, still attracts clicks and lets me fit more information in the sidebar.

Generally, bigger advertising boxes attract more clicks (duh!) but you don't want to overwhelm your audience with ads. The graphic shows the click-through rate by ad sizes compared to a 468x60 banner ad. The 300x250 size box is displayed as "medium rectangle" in the chart.

Larger Ad Units Generate Higher Click Rates

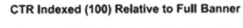

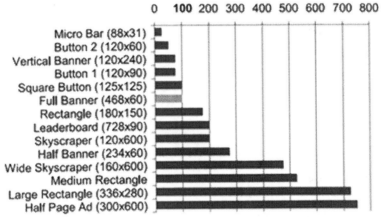

The way advertising works is that companies pay for their ads to show when a keyword is searched or around content that is relevant to that keyword. Google studies your blog to see what you write about and places ads on the site for which your readers may be interested.

Blogs around health, insurance, finance and travel generally benefit from higher advertising rates. There's big money in these industries and companies pay to advertise their products and services. This doesn't mean you should force yourself or your blog into one of these topics. Talking about something in which you have no interest will take more time to write and will only lead to burnout.

It's important here to note that you should never click on the ads on your own site or ask other people to click. Google is really good at seeing which clicks are genuinely through interest and which are fake clicks. If it finds you are clicking ads on your site or asking others to, it will ban you from Adsense and it will be nearly impossible to get back in the program.

It varies a little but about one in every hundred page views will result in a click on one of your ads. Your blog's topic will determine how much you make from each click, but the average here seems to be between $0.75 and $1.25 click.

If you are making about $1 per click and you get approximately one click per hundred page views (1% CTR) then you will be making roughly $0.01 per page view. These are not numbers I pulled out of thin air but the actual statistics from my own Adsense account and inline with what I've seen on other personal finance blogs.

One penny per page view is not something that is going to put you in the 10% of bloggers making more than $15,000 a month blogging. **Sponsored posts are a strong revenue stream for bloggers** but it may take some time to develop.

Because of the horrible click-through-rates of advertising, content marketing has emerged as a more effective way to get a product or service in front of an audience. Content marketing is stealthier than direct advertising. A blogger writes about a topic that is of interest to the audience. That topic may be about a problem the audience has or just something they'd be interested in learning more about.

What the audience may not know is that the article is written to persuade readers to use a specific company's product or service. One or more links are included in the article that direct back to the company or a product landing page.

Native Advertising Roundup did a 2014 survey that showed 73% of advertisers had paid for sponsored posts and 93% expected to do so in the future. Sponsored posts, also called native advertising and content marketing, and are expected to grow from $1.3 billion in 2013 to $9.4 billion by the end of 2018.

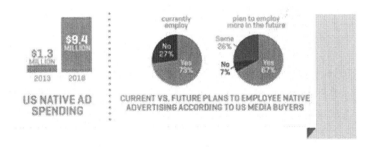

There is a fine line between accepting sponsored content on your blog and alienating readers by being a shill for anyone that will pay you. You should always be honest about your assessment of a product and only accept the paid content if you are comfortable using the product or service yourself.

Since sponsored content is paid on a single article on a single page, you likely will not get many offers or be able to sell the idea to advertisers until you build a decent amount of traffic for your blog. Advertisers are not going to want to pay much if their message is only seen by a few hundred people. Once you are seeing upwards of 10,000 visitors a month to your blog, it is time to start approaching advertisers for sponsored content.

Where do you find advertisers for sponsored content? Writing in your blog's topic for even a few months should give you a good idea of who sells products and services in the niche. You can check out your Google Adsense account to see which ads and companies show up frequently. You may even see sponsored content show up on other blogs in the same topic.

After finding your targets for sponsored posts, you'll need to put together a pitch for why they should advertise through sponsored content on your blog. You can informally pitch them the idea through a quick email but I've found that a formal presentation goes a long way to getting the deal done.

Within your pitch, you will want to highlight:

- Keywords for which you rank on the front page of Google – focusing on those relevant to the advertiser

- Blog site statistics including: monthly unique visitors, page views, the percentage of visitors from specific countries, bounce rate, time on page and pages per visitor

- The percentage of your traffic from organic search, social media and referral

- Number of social media followers and any sharing statistics you have for prior posts

- Your domain authority and Alexa rank

- The age of your blog and number of email subscribers

When negotiating the sponsored content with an advertiser, it's important to detail:

- How many words they expect for the content

- How many links will be included in the content

- Whether the paid content will be a flat-fee or based on the number of page views

- If the company requires editing authority before the post goes live

- How many times the article will be promoted through your blog's social media network or through the newsletter

- How many articles will be written and the posting frequency

While there is no standard price for sponsored content, I have seen some research on pricing. MOZ published a great study in 2015 of 474 blogs using sponsored content. The most common price, just over 40% of posts, was $100 while some bloggers charged as high as $500 per post.

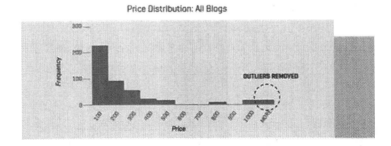

Price Distribution: All Blogs

The study found that most blogs charged between $100 and $200 for sponsored content and that is probably where you should start.

I would not recommend running more than three or four sponsored content articles per month. It depends on how overt you are promoting the sponsor's product or service. If the article is useful information without pushing readers to the product, you may be able to run more sponsored articles without appearing to be selling out to sponsors.

Just four sponsored content articles a month could add up to $800 or more for your blog. You may not get much until your blog reaches a certain level of readership but it is definitely a revenue stream you want to approach.

It is more difficult to estimate how much you can make from sponsored content, on a per page view basis. How much a blog makes varies quite a bit by the amount of time a blogger spends seeking sponsors and month-to-month blog statistics. I know several bloggers with sites that get over 25,000 page views per month and make between $0.02 and $0.05 per page view on sponsored content by charging $150 per post.

True Passive Potential: Blogging

Blogging is likely the biggest passive income myth out there and anyone that has ever tried running a successful blog will tell you it is not a road to riches...unless they are trying to sell you their 10-step secret formula to blogging riches!

The draw of blogging comes from its extremely low cost. You can launch a blog on less than $100 for hosting, domain registration, and some other costs. Ongoing costs can add up depending on how much support and add-ons you want for the blog but generally costs are very low compared to other passive income investments.

The drawback to blogging, and what makes it a poor choice for true passive income, is that it requires a high time commitment. You will spend a minimum of a couple hours on each post; between writing, sourcing images, and optimizing for search engines. You should spend at least a few hours a week promoting your blog through social media and through blogger networks. A successful blog will also require a couple of hours responding to comments and reader emails.

Cash flow on blogs is also low compared to other passive income investments. While your return on the money invested in your blog may be high, as long as you don't spend much, the cash return on your time spent will be next to nothing for at least a year.

Income continuity is rather low for blogs. While a successful blog will continue to attract readers through search well after you have stopped contributing, the income will start to decline. Given enough income, you can outsource blog administration to make it a true source of passive income but it will take time to generate that level of income to pay for running the entire blog.

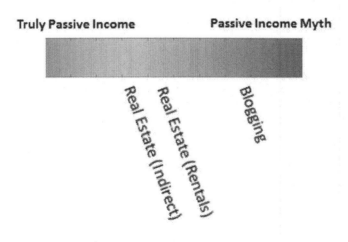

Passive Income Potential Scale

Overall, blogging is a poor source of passive income though it can be a great profession and a good source of active income. The benefits from blogging include pride of ownership and editorial control over your own work, as well as other non-monetary benefits. You can blog from anywhere in the world, giving you the freedom to travel or live where you like.

Online Stores

Growth in online spending hit $20 billion in 2014 and shows no sign of slowing. Expectations for online shopping to reach nearly $44 billion over the next few years has people pushing to get in line for their share of the profits. As part of that frenzy, one of the greatest passive income myths has been born – all you need to do is put out the sign on your online store and wait for the masses to give you their money.

Running an online store can be part of your blog, adding an additional revenue source, or it can be a stand-alone source of income.

Like blogging though, online stores may be a poor source of passive income.

Online Stores and Passive Income

The graphic, courtesy of eMarketer Research, shows total U.S. retail sales as well as ecommerce sales for the two years through 2014 and then expectations through 2018. While traditional (offline) retail sales are expected to grow about 5% annually over the five-year period, online retail sales are expected to jump 23.4% over the same period.

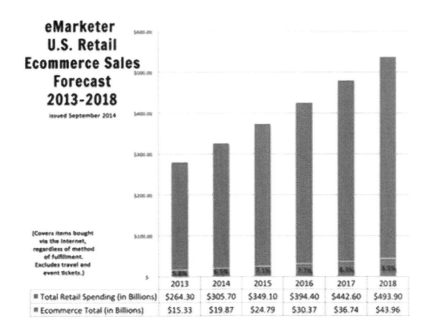

eMarketer U.S. Retail Ecommerce Sales Forecast 2013-2018	2013	2014	2015	2016	2017	2018
▪ Total Retail Spending (in Billions)	$264.30	$305.70	$349.10	$394.40	$442.60	$493.90
▪ Ecommerce Total (in Billions)	$15.33	$19.87	$24.79	$30.37	$36.74	$43.96

Besides the faster growth in online spending, e-tailers don't have the high start-up costs of opening a brick-and-mortar store. There are no rental leases or utility bills for an online store. You don't have to get up at the crack of dawn to open the door, hoping that someone finds your shop.

Just as with blogging, the success stories have helped perpetuate the myth that riches await through your online storefront.

By selling affiliate products, you don't even need to create something of your own to sell! Just post a picture and a link of someone else's product and let the money roll in.

The reality of an online store, as we saw with blogging, is that they are easy to set up but success takes a bit more work. In fact, your online store is likely to provide even less passive income than blogging.

Let's look at the two ways you make money from an online store then how to set one up.

Affiliate Sales for Passive Income

Affiliate sales are a lot like the advertising we saw in blogging but you only get paid if someone actually buys a product or service. A lot of companies offer commissions on sales of their products. To take advantage of this, you sign up directly on the company's website or through an affiliate network like Flexoffers or Amazon Associates.

Once you've signed up for the program, you get a special URL link and images of products. Whether on your blog or in your online store, you place a picture and a description of a product along with the URL link from the affiliate program. If someone clicks through the link and then buys the product, you receive a flat-fee or percentage commission on the sale.

While pay-per-click advertising normally pays just pennies or a few bucks per click, affiliate sales can pay hundreds of dollars on each sale. Of course, the drawback is that affiliate sales happen much less frequently than do clicks on advertising banners.

If you figure only about 1% of the pageviews to a webpage result in a click on an advertisement or an affiliate ad, and maybe 5% are actually going to buy the product from the ad, you would need 2,000 pageviews to get one affiliate sale! (2,000 pageviews * 1% * 5% = 1 affiliate sale)

How much you make for affiliate ads varies quite a bit. Amazon pays between 1% and 10% on sales of products from people you send over through an affiliate link. That isn't much if someone is buying an ebook or some electronics gear. I've seen other affiliate programs, especially those for loans and website hosting, pay $100 or more for each sale.

Using an approximate of $50 for each affiliate sale and 2,000 page views for each sale leads to estimated earnings of $0.025 per page view. That's pretty good compared to standard click advertising so a popular way to earn an income.

To improve their chance at an affiliate sale, most bloggers will write an article reviewing the product. This is really just a combination of the sponsored post and advertising strategy we saw in the previous chapter. Writing specifically about the product is more likely to attract visitors from Google search that might be interested in a purchase.

Much like sponsored content, you have to be careful with content around affiliate promotions. If the product or service is of poor quality, you risk alienating your readers by writing a glowing recommendation. There are plenty of affiliate programs out there in any niche, so there is really no need to push a specific product. Most of the bloggers I know insist on trying the product first and then decide whether they want to endorse it through an article.

This can be an added bonus to blogging or running a successful online store. I have seen blogs that receive upwards of $500 a month in free merchandise just so the blogger will review the product.

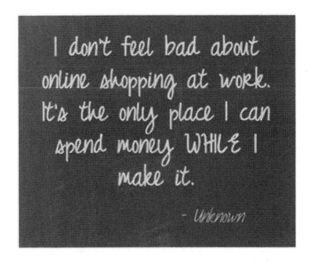

I don't feel bad about online shopping at work. It's the only place I can spend money WHILE I make it.

- Unknown

Selling your Own Products Online

Selling your own products or services through a blog or online store is arguably the best way to make money online. You are only making a slim cut on advertising after the ad network has taken its share. The same is true for affiliate sales and sponsored content but selling your own product puts you first in line for profits.

Unfortunately, selling your own products or services means you need something to sell. Manufacturing a product can cost thousands in upfront expenses. Creating a book could take months to write and will cost money to edit and finish. Even selling consulting services means you have to establish yourself as an expert and then spend the time consulting.

How much you make on your products can vary. Books are relatively easy to sell but do not make much money for each sale. I spend an average of $2,250 in editing and production for each book I produce and most sell for between $3.99 and $7.99 per copy. Sales through your own website will net you the full list price while those through Amazon or Createspace (for print-on-demand) will net you between 30% and 70% of the list price.

I generally sell between 35 and 75 copies of each book per month through my websites and Amazon. I change list prices sometimes to boost sales but generally make about $200 a month. That's not much but can build to a decent source of income if you've got three or four books.

My own experience and talking with other bloggers is that product sales generally earn between $0.01 to $0.05 per page view.

How to Setup and Manage an Online Store

While a lot of the bloggers I know sell affiliate products or their own stuff through their personal blog, you can also sell products through a separate online store. The dream of passive income riches has led to an industry of platforms that make it quick and easy to put up your own digital storefront.

We'll look at the process for setting up an online store on the Shopify platform though it's pretty much the same with most platforms.

Shopify is an online retail hosting platform, a website that offers the ability to host your own website on top of its system. Think of Shopify as Amazon meets WordPress. With Shopify, you can create an online store as well as a full website or blog with your own domain name.

The process of creating an online store through Shopify is fairly simple. You choose a theme from one of the 100+ templates including themes designed for specific industries like fashion, jewelry or electronics. Just as with a blog, the theme is the layout of the website. You can customize themes with different colors and fonts as well as adding your own logo.

Shopify is integrated with payment processors like PayPal and Authorize.net, which makes payment processing easier. If you are setting up an online store on your own blog, you'll need a merchant account and an SSL certificate to process payments.

There are three monthly subscription levels on Shopify from $29 up to $179 for the unlimited features. The professional and unlimited plans offer a few extra reporting and tracking options but most new store owners do just fine on the basic plan.

BASIC	PROFESSIONAL	UNLIMITED
$29/mo	$79/mo	$179/mo
Try Shopify for free	Try Shopify for free	Try Shopify for free
CREDIT CARD RATE	**CREDIT CARD RATE**	**CREDIT CARD RATE**
Online: 2.9% + 30¢	Online: 2.6% + 30¢	Online: 2.4% + 30¢
In Person: 2.7% + 0¢	In Person: 2.4% + 0¢	In Person: 2.2% + 0¢
FEATURES	**FEATURES**	**FEATURES**
Shopify POS	Shopify POS	Shopify POS
1 GB file storage	5 GB file storage	Unlimited file storage
Unlimited products	Unlimited products	Unlimited products
24/7 Support	24/7 Support	24/7 Support
Discount code engine	Discount code engine	Discount code engine
No transaction fees	No transaction fees	No transaction fees
Fraud analysis tools	Fraud analysis tools	Fraud analysis tools
Gift cards	Gift cards	Gift cards
Professional reports	Professional reports	Professional reports
Abandoned cart recovery	Abandoned cart recovery	Abandoned cart recovery
Advanced report builder	Advanced report builder	Advanced report builder
Real-time carrier shipping	Real-time carrier shipping	Real-time carrier shipping

From the administration area on your Shopify account, you will add products and manage inventory. Adding products is a matter of uploading images and writing product descriptions.

Professional quality pictures are a must for products so you might want to, at minimum, invest in a camera that can take high resolution pictures. You also want to write detailed and keyword-rich descriptions of your products. Not only will it help convert visitors to buyers but it will help get your store found in search results.

Besides selling your own products, you can also sell affiliate products through a Shopify store. To sell affiliate products, you upload an image and description just as you would your own products. You can include your affiliate link so buyers click directly through and make the purchase.

While setting up an online store is quick and costs next to nothing, the dream of passive income from an online retail operation is far from reality. Much like we saw in blogging, an online store without something to drive virtual customers to it isn't going to make any money. You need to give people a reason to visit your store. With only a fraction of the visitors likely to actually buy anything, you need a lot of people to visit your store to make any real money.

Getting People to your Online Store

Drawing people to your online store is either through organic promotion, through blogging and Google search, or through external promotion.

We covered blogging in the previous chapter so will focus on external promotion. External promotion of your online store is marketing through other blogs, direct advertising or through social media. You can do this without managing your own blog but a lot of people combine the two methods, using external promotion to get things going until their own blog builds momentum.

Guest posting on other blogs is a great way to draw visitors to your own blog and can be helpful in bringing people to an online store. While many bloggers will accept a guest post from another blog, they might charge a fee for a guest post that links directly to an online store.

Social media is the most popular way of promoting online stores, both through direct advertising and through free outreach to followers. Building a following large enough to drive traffic to your online store usually means a few years of developing a social network. Becoming overly promotional to your store risks alienating those friends and fans pretty quick so a lot of people create different accounts for their store and for their personal lives.

True Passive Income Potential: Online Stores

With some minor differences, online stores are very similar to blogging and the passive income potential is nearly identical. Blogging offers the advantage of being able to place advertisements and sponsored content on your blog. You will still have to respond to customer questions and emails with an online store but ongoing management may be a little easier compared to a blog since you are not constantly creating content articles.

Online stores are generally inexpensive to set up and manage but costs can build quickly if you focus on external paid promotion rather than blogging or using your social network. A basic Shopify plan will cost $29 per month and includes everything you need to get started including a hosting plan.

The problem with online stores, relative to blogging, is that once you stop promoting the store through paid advertisement or content then traffic declines immediately. The lingering traffic from search for a blog does not apply to an online store unless you have a blog associated with it. This means that online stores may be an even poorer choice for passive income unless you earn enough to outsource promotion of your store.

Time commitment is slightly lower for an online store compared to blogging but still high relative to other passive income investments. Income momentum and continuity are also both extremely low for an online store relative to other passive income strategies. There is almost no momentum from previous sales unless you can convert prior customers to repeat buyers and the store will require continuous promotion to generate new sales.

Passive Income Potential Scale

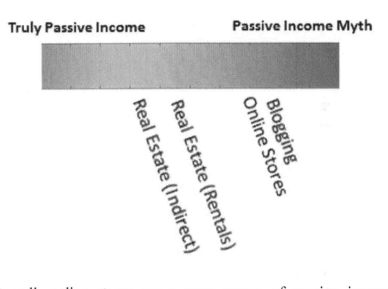

Overall, online stores are a poor source of passive income though they can be good sources of active income, especially when combined with a blog. Online spending is increasing and running a virtual storefront is much cheaper than managing a traditional retail establishment. Combining an online store with a blog allows you to take advantage of four different streams of revenue through advertising, sponsored content, affiliate products and sales of your own products.

Income Investing

Income investing through dividend stocks and master limited partnerships (MLPs) is closer to the true intent of building a passive income than the previous strategies we've covered. While start-up costs are considerably higher to build a high income, the time it takes to see cash flow is considerably lower and there is little ongoing work to be done to continue reaping the rewards. There are still risks involved though and the returns on income investing can be lower than that of other income strategies.

While income investing through dividend-paying stocks is the most popular among investors, there are other investments that offer good passive income potential including master limited partnerships and real estate investment trusts (REITs). We will cover dividend stocks and MLPs in this chapter since REITs were covered in the chapter on indirect real estate investing.

I have been an investment analyst for nearly a decade now and have seen income investing strategies come and go. Income investing, especially within retirement planning, is one of the most popular investing topics and attracts a lot of get-rich-quick schemes. Investors get drawn into trading schemes by the promise of high income and the potential for price returns on stocks. What they get is sub-par returns and income that fails to live up to the hype.

Reading through the chapter, pick up the larger picture of how these investments are able to pay out strong cash flows. Use a few simple criteria to pick income stocks with solid futures and do not overcomplicate investing with ridiculous trading strategies.

Dividend Investing

Running a business means regularly making the decision between investing profits back into the business for growth or cashing out some of those profits to the owners. For smaller companies, the opportunities for growth outweigh the short-term benefit of a cash return to owners. As the company matures and growth opportunities become scarcer, the scale shifts to favor returning some of the cash to owners. When a company has issued shares, it returns that cash in the form of dividends to stock owners.

Understanding the trade-off between dividends and growth will help you avoid falling for hype in some dividend investing scams. If the company is returning a large chunk of earnings to investors as a dividend, then it's likely that opportunities to grow the business will be limited. Be cautious anytime someone promise you a high dividend yield stock that is projected to grow at double-digit rates per year.

For most companies, dividends are paid every three months according to a fixed amount for every share you own. There are companies that pay dividends twice or once a year, or even twelve times a year but these are the exception rather than the rule.

Investing in these companies that pay regular dividends is likely the most popular passive income strategy. Depending on how much you have invested in dividend-paying companies and how much the company pays per share, you can build a strong income without having to do much of anything.

I myself have a lot of my portfolio invested in dividend stocks. The companies tend to be more mature and less prone to huge price swings. As an investment analyst, much of my annual income is tied to stock market performance so I balance that risk by taking less risk in my own investments.

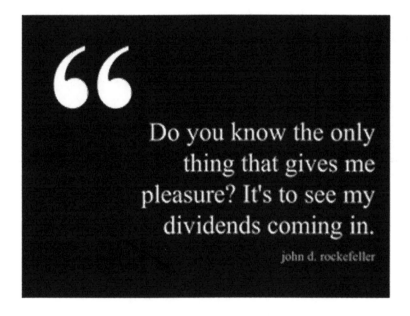

Do you know the only thing that gives me pleasure? It's to see my dividends coming in.

john d. rockefeller

How to Create a Passive Income Dividend Strategy

Picking strong dividend stocks for a passive income strategy is actually easier than you might believe. Behind all the commentary on TV and the analysis are really five criteria: dividend yield, payout ratio, price-earnings ratio, operating margin and diversification. Using these five qualifiers will help you put together a portfolio of stocks that will create a stable income stream for years to come.

Understanding some of the basic terminology will help us get started in setting up a passive income dividend strategy.

A stock's **dividend yield** is just the annual dividend divided by the price of the shares. If the company pays a $1 dividend each quarter ($4 per year) and the stock price is $120 then the yield would be 3.3% ($4/$120 = 0.033). The dividend yield is how much cash return the stock is going to provide every year. It may increase or decrease slightly depending on movement in the share price but most companies try to maintain a fairly consistent yield.

 DIVIDEND YIELD = ANNUAL DIVIDEND / SHARE PRICE

The **payout ratio** is the percentage of a company's profit or net income it pays out as dividends. If a company earns $20 per share over a year's period and pays out $12 in dividends then the payout ratio is 60% ($12 divided by $20 = 0.60). The payout ratio is important because it reflects how much the company is keeping back to reinvest in growth. A company that pays out nearly everything in dividends may not be able to grow the business, or the stock price. I generally limit my search to companies that pay between 30% and 70% of their income as dividends. This ensures that management is serious about returning profits to shareholders but also wants to keep the business growing.

PAYOUT RATIO = TOTAL DIVIDENDS PAID / NET INCOME

Dividend stocks in the S&P 500, the largest U.S.-based companies, pay an average dividend yield around 2% though it ranges from less than a percent to well into double-digit yields. Stocks with a yield below 2% probably will not be very attractive to an income investor while stocks offering yields above 10% may not be able to support the payment. I would stick with stocks that pay between 3% and 6% on an annual basis. This provides for a good cash return but avoids being drawn in to stocks on super-high dividends only to see the cash return cut.

There are more than 800 publicly listed companies that trade on the New York Stock Exchange, the Nasdaq and the American Stock Exchange that pay dividends. I have made a living as an equity analyst, working with fund managers to pick the best investments but the best strategy is often the most simple.

A simple stock screener tool will get you started with nearly everything you need. I like starting with dividend stocks that yield over 3% and that have made payments for at least five years. You can check dividend payments on Yahoo Finance by clicking on the *Historical Prices* link in the left-side menu.

From the initial list, I also look for companies that pay out between 30% and 70% of their income as dividends. The payout ratio is also available on Yahoo Finance by clicking *Key Statistics* and then scrolling down to the lower-right under *Dividends & Splits*.

Using just these two criteria is still going to leave you with a large list of potential dividend stocks in which to invest. I generally also limit my search by companies with a market capitalization, the value of all shares, of at least $5 billion to make sure I am looking at large companies with some financial power behind them.

I also compare the **price-to-earnings (PE) ratio** and **operating margin** among stocks within each sector and industry. The PE ratio is just the stock's price divided by the company's net income over the last four quarters. It is a crude measure because management often uses tactics to manipulate earnings but it is easily understood and can give a passable idea of value.

The operating margin is the earnings after operating expenses divided by sales, a good measure for how well management is running the company. The PE ratio and operating margin are relative measures, meaning they are only useful when compared against the stock's historical average or against other stocks.

Which brings us to one of the most important ideas in dividend investing, more important than picking individual stocks with high dividends and reasonable payout ratios, **you absolutely must pick stocks from different sectors and industries.**

Every company in the stock market belongs to an industry which shares a relatively common product type. Google, Yahoo and Facebook are all website companies within the internet information providers industry. Industries that share common characteristics are grouped into sectors like technology, healthcare or energy.

Structure of the Stock Market

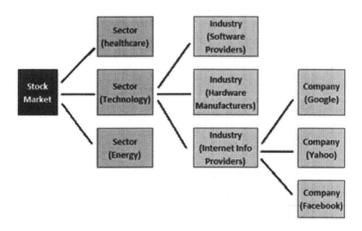

The reason this is important, especially when building your portfolio, is that each sector reacts differently to the economy and other market forces. The utilities sector reacts negatively to higher interest rates because cash flows to public utilities are mostly fixed while higher interest rates are generally a good thing for companies in the financials sector.

Calm down, you don't really have to become an economist to figure out how each sector reacts differently or to build a dividend stock portfolio. The key idea here is that you understand the need to make sure you have a good mix of stocks from each sector. That way, when the economy or news headlines are playing havoc with a specific sector, you'll have stocks in the other eight sectors to keep your portfolio steady.

It can be a lot to take in but you don't have to be an expert overnight. A simple strategy of picking stocks from a few criteria and from each of the sectors, holding them for at least five to ten years is generally best. Resist the urge to "buy-low and sell-high" or to listen to brokers with a hot tip.

- Be wary of stocks with dividend yields of 10% or higher. It might just be a function of a falling stock price and weak outlook for the company. The dividend is likely unsustainable and could be cut.

- Make sure you hold at least 20 stocks in your portfolio and no one stock should account for more than 10% of your total wealth. That way, even a total loss in one stock will not devastate your investments.

- Don't forget stocks of foreign companies for international diversification.

- Putting all your money in stocks leaves you at risk of another market crash, no matter how diversified you are in different sectors. A well-rounded portfolio includes fixed income, real estate investments, and other strategies.

An Alternative to Investing in Individual Companies

One popular alternative to buying dividend stocks of individual companies is to buy shares of exchange traded funds (ETFs). These are like mutual funds, where a manager buys individual stocks and then allows you to invest in the entire portfolio with just one purchase. While most people are more familiar with mutual funds, I prefer ETFs for several reasons:

- ETFs trade on the stock exchanges just like stocks. You can buy and sell them easily and commissions are usually very low. Mutual funds do not trade during the day so the price you get when you buy or sell isn't known until the end of the day.

- ETFs are usually much cheaper than mutual funds. Mutual funds may charge expense fees of 2% or higher and up to 5% to buy and sell the fund. ETFs normally charge expense fees of less than 1% and you can buy or sell shares for as little as $5 with an online investing platform.

There are thousands of ETFs. Some invest in stocks, others in bonds and still others that invest in real estate, commodities and any other investments.

For dividend investing, check out these three ETFs:

- iShares International Select Dividend (NYSE: IDV) provides exposure to 103 companies in non-U.S. developed markets and pays a 4.9% dividend yield

- iShares Emerging Markets Dividend (NYSE: DVYE) provides exposure to 102 companies in emerging markets and pays a 4.1% dividend yield

- Vanguard High Dividend Yield (NYSE: VYM) holds stock in 435 U.S.-based companies and pays a 2.9% dividend yield

Returns to a Passive Income Dividend Strategy

With bonds paying next to nothing on historically low interest rates, dividends have become the next best thing for income investors looking for stability and safety. While you'll find newer companies that pay dividends, most are relatively large and mature corporations with less volatility than the average stock.

Dividends have historically accounted for about a third of the total return on stocks and sometimes as much as half of the return when the market tumbles. The change is mostly due to the ups and downs in prices against the stability of dividends. While price appreciation amounted to a bigger slice of the market return in the 90s, many investors didn't have a chance to book those returns before the internet bubble sent prices crashing.

Components of Monthly Total Return on S&P 500

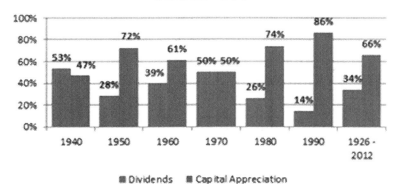

Source: Dow Jones S&P Indices LLC

Not only is dividend investing an important part of the overall return to stocks but dividend-paying companies have historically beaten other stocks on return. Over the four decades to 2012, dividend-paying stocks that regularly increased their dividends returned 9.5% on an annual basis compared to a return of just 1.6% for stocks of companies that paid no dividends. Even companies that did not increase their dividend payment offered a 7.2% annual return over the period.

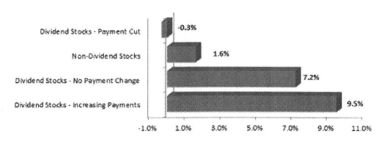

Source: Ned Davis Research - based on monthly equal-weighted geometric average, reconstituted monthly

There is a good reason why dividend stocks tend to outperform other stocks. Paying out a regular dividend requires cash management and spending discipline, something that a lot of corporate management lacks. The need to consistently pay and even increase the dividend means that management needs to be more selective of the projects it wants to support.

Over a long period of investing in dividend stocks, you should see between 2% and 4% annual return from dividends along with about 3% or 6% return on the share price. A cash return of 3% is likely not going to be enough to cover all your expenses if you are living off dividends as a source of passive income but it is a return for which you really didn't have to do much to earn.

Younger investors will want to reinvest their dividend payments to buy more shares, building the portfolio and potential income for the future. Older investors may need to gradually sell some of their shares to supplement dividend payments and cover living expenses.

Risks to a Passive Income Dividend Strategy

The biggest risk to a passive income dividend strategy is that the company will cut its dividend payment or will not have the cash flow to grow the dividend. A dividend that doesn't grow over the years will not help you much against the constant loss to inflation and lower purchasing power. Holding a diversified group of dividend stocks, across different sectors will help avoid problems related to larger economic issues. With the drop in oil prices at the end of 2014, many energy companies rushed to protect cash flow and cut their dividends but payments in other sectors like healthcare remained stable.

Choosing stocks of companies with advantages in size also helps avoid problems with dividend growth. It's not to say that giants like General Electric cannot fall on hard times but the company is less likely to run out of cash than companies that don't benefit from worldwide scale and billions in cash reserves.

Another risk to your passive income dividend strategy is the difference between qualified and non-qualified dividends. The distinction isn't well known among investors but can save you a ton of money at tax time. Qualified dividends are taxed at a lower rate, and may be tax free for investors in lower income brackets. Non-qualified dividends are taxed at your personal income rate which can eat into nearly half the return for high-income investors.

To make sure your dividends are 'qualified' you need to hold the shares for at least 61 days within the 121-day period around the date when the dividend was declared by the company. This usually isn't a problem for most investors but you'll want to take note if you sell your dividend stocks frequently.

Required Holding Periods to Earn Qualified Dividends

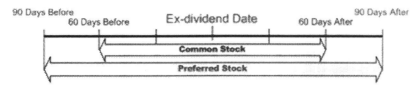

MLP Investing

As we saw with real estate investment trusts (REITs), the government has allowed tax advantages on certain types of investments. As difficult as it is to "beat" the market and earn a respectable rate of return on a portfolio, these tax breaks make for opportunities that you just cannot pass up.

Anytime a company can avoid corporate taxes while managing a certain type of investment or you can avoid income taxes on your investments, returns should naturally be higher compared to the taxed alternative.

Master Limited Partnerships (MLPs) are another type of tax-advantaged investment structure that actually benefits from avoidance of corporate taxes and personal income taxes. It's a combination you do not want to ignore.

What are Master Limited Partnerships?

MLPs are a special business structure that combines the benefits of a corporation with the tax advantages of a partnership. Since 1981, the U.S. Congress has allowed these businesses to avoid paying corporate income taxes if 90% or more of their income was passed through to the partners.

In 1987, Congress restricted MLPs to those companies in the energy, real estate or finance sectors. Most real estate firms have opted to go with the REIT structure, which is similar. As of December 2013, most (84%) of MLPs were in the energy sector.

MLP market capitalization: $491.3 billion   Energy MLP market capitalization: $413.5 billion

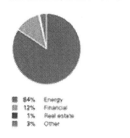
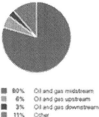

- 84% Energy
- 12% Financial
- 1%   Real estate
- 3%   Other

- 80% Oil and gas midstream
- 6%   Oil and gas upstream
- 3%   Oil and gas downstream
- 11% Other

Source: Vanguard Research 2014

Further, most energy MLPs (80%) are in the midstream segment of the sector.

- Energy companies in the upstream segment are involved in exploration and drilling for oil & natural gas. They are "upstream" or removed furthest from the retail customers.

- Energy companies in the midstream segment are involved in transportation and storage of energy through pipelines and storage facilities.

- Energy companies in the downstream segment are involved in refining, i.e. turning oil into usable products like gasoline, and selling products to customers.

Midstream energy companies own pipeline and storage facilities and typically get paid for volume of oil or gas that they transport. This is an important point because it removes some of the risk around oil & gas prices. Midstream MLPs may do well even when energy prices are falling because they are paid on the amount of energy demanded rather than the price.

As a result of the tax benefits to the MLP structure, many energy companies have sold their pipeline and storage assets to an MLP. The energy company gets cash for the assets and the MLP can manage them more efficiently, without having to pay taxes.

MLPs are generally controlled by a General Partner (GP) and often don't even have employees. The MLP simply is a company structure to own the pipelines and storage facilities while the GP manages them by contracting with companies for transportation and storage. The GP takes a fee for management and sometimes an incentive percentage of profits.

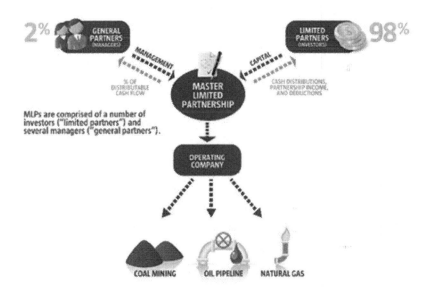

In addition to the corporate tax benefits, MLP investors also benefit on their own income taxes. Since MLP investors are partners in the assets, they not only get passed through the earnings but also the tax benefits from depreciation of the pipeline and storage infrastructure. Remember that with REITs, the company benefits by being able to write off the annual amount of real estate depreciation before it passes earnings on to investors.

MLPs pass these depreciation benefits directly through to investors, which use the depreciation to offset the income they receive from the MLPs. As a result, investors generally pay current year taxes only on a small portion (usually 10% to 20%) of the income they receive from the MLP.

The other side to this is that the amount offset by depreciation lowers your cost in the investment. That means you pay higher taxes when you sell the investment. When you sell an MLP investment, a portion of the gain will be taxed as income rather than capital gains.

There is one way around this though...never sell your MLP investments. These are investments in real assets, energy pipelines and storage, which will be around for decades and in constant demand. Best yet, if an MLP investment is passed on through an estate, your heirs will not have to pay the taxes you owed. The cost of the shares is marked up to the point where they inherited the investment and all the taxes owed are wiped out.

One downside to MLP investments is the special tax form you will receive every year, called a schedule K-1 form. This form lists out the income, deductions, losses and credits on the partnership. This helps to calculate how much of your income is taxable after depreciation. Some investors find it difficult, or at least a hassle, to work through the K-1 form and transfer the amounts to their taxes. Any tax accountant should easily be able to handle the forms though they may charge a little extra. Most tax software packages have a relatively easy walk-through to putting your MLP investments on your taxes.

Why invest in MLPs?

The tax advantages of MLPs have helped them outperform other investments in the past. The graphic shows the returns to MLP investments compared to stocks, bonds and Treasury bonds. Over nearly two decades since 1996, MLPs have offered a total annual return of about 15% versus 8.6% on stocks and 5.6% on corporate bonds.

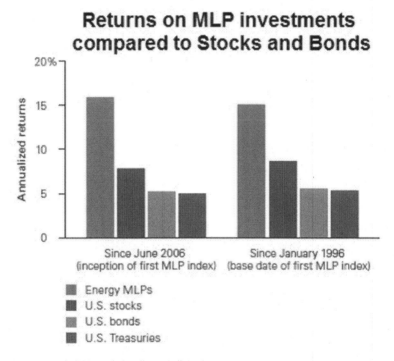

Source: Vanguard Research, 2014

For income investors, MLPs offer some of the highest payouts in investing. As of year-end 2013, energy MLPs offered an average yield of 5.5%; compared to 4.4% for REITs, 2% for stocks and 2.5% for bonds. The higher income and deferred tax advantages make MLPs some of the most preferred investments for people living off their investment income.

How to Create a Stream of Income from MLPs

MLP investments trade just like regular stocks and can be bought cheaply through online investing sites like E*Trade or TD Ameritrade. Technically, your investment in an MLP is for "units" of the partnership rather than stock and the income you receive is called "distributions" rather than "dividends." There is really no difference though and only the purists will be annoyed if you call it stocks or dividends.

As with REITs, some of the popular measures for stocks like the price-earnings ratio are not applicable for MLP investments. Instead, MLP investors primarily use two metrics called Distributable Cash Flow (DCF) and the Coverage Ratio.

Distributable cash flow measures the partnership's ability to generate cash after expenses and costs to maintain the business. Since MLPs return most of their annual cash to investors, it is a measure of how much is available to shareholders.

Calculating DCF is straight-forward and just involves adding back non-cash items like depreciation back to net income. These items are removed from net income on the company's income statement for tax reporting purposes but do not represent an actual outflow of cash. Maintenance capital expenditures are the annual amount spent to keep all the pipelines or storage facilities operating normally. Removing this amount leaves you with how much cash the company could distribute without having to worry about infrastructure wearing out and losing business. Most partnerships will calculate DCF for you in their financial statements.

MLP Investing: Calculating DCF

	Net Income
+	Depreciation, Depletion & Amortization
+	Other Non-Cash Items
-	Maintenance Capital Expenditures
equals	**Distributable Cash Flow (DCF)**

The coverage ratio is another important measure. While partnerships could distribute all their DCF, it is safer to retain some cash for future growth or spending. The coverage ratio is the DCF divided by the amount the partnership actually distributed over the last year.

COVERAGE RATIO = DCF / CASH DISTRIBUTED TO INVESTORS

When analyzing different MLP investments, you want to make sure the distributable cash flow is increasing at a fairly steady rate. This means the partnership is doing a good job of generating more cash to return to investors. You also want to make sure the company is returning cash but not too much by looking at the coverage ratio. There's no rule but I like to make sure the company has a coverage ratio of at least 1.2 times (DCF divided by distributed cash = 1.2).

Looking at different MLP investments, you will also want to pay attention to how much the General Partner benefits from its management. Besides a fee, usually around 2%, many general partners get special payouts called Incentive Distribution Rights (IDRs). These IDRs give the general partner the right to an increasing percentage of the cash flow depending on the distribution per unit. It favors the general partner over investors and many investor groups have fought against the practice. Some MLPs have started to manage their own assets or pay the general partner a fixed-amount instead of a percentage.

Long-term investors do not generally have to worry too much about picking the perfect MLP investment. Invest equally across a group of five to 10 different MLPs with relatively stable increases in DCF and good coverage ratios. This will help smooth out your total investment returns even if one MLP stumbles. Do not sell out of your MLP investments. Hold your MLP investments forever and enjoy the tax benefit.

Since MLPs are almost exclusively energy companies, keep an eye on your total exposure to stocks and bonds of energy companies. Holding 10% of your portfolio in MLPs may not seem like you are exposed to weakness in energy prices but factoring in your 10% holding of energy stocks like Exxon Mobil and another 5% holding of bonds from energy companies presents a different picture.

While there are exchange traded funds (ETFs) that hold MLP company shares, just as there are ETFs for REIT investing, I do not generally recommend them. Investment in MLP funds will avoid getting the K-1 form every year for your taxes but the funds do not enjoy the same tax benefits. Regulatory requirements mean that most MLP funds have to register as regular corporations, meaning they pay corporate taxes on their profits. Losing out on the tax advantage means that MLP funds underperform direct investing in individual MLPs every year. On your side, you will pay regular income taxes on the full amount of income you receive from the fund.

FORMULA FOR SUCCESS: RISE EARLY, WORK HARD, STRIKE OIL.

~j. paul getty

Risks and Return on MLP Investments

As with any sector, MLP companies are prone to overbuilding over a period only to face overcapacity afterwards. We have not yet seen this because of the surging demand for oil & gas pipelines and the revolution in U.S. energy production. Even on lower prices recently, energy production is likely to keep increasing in the United States for quite some time.

While MLPs generally get paid on the volume of energy they transport or store, they still carry some risk on lower energy prices. There are a couple of reasons for this, besides the fact that some revenue is tied to the price of oil or gas. Falling energy prices may weaken investor sentiment for all types of energy investments including MLPs. Uncertainty in the energy sector due to falling prices makes it more difficult for MLPs to secure funding and contracts for services.

MLP investments carry some interest rate risk, similar to what we saw in REIT investments. Because the companies pay out almost all income each year, they must continually find new funding by issuing bonds or selling stock units. If interest rates go up, it becomes more expensive to issue debt and interest expense will increase. If interest rates keep rising, the partnership may issue more unit shares instead of debt, which dilutes your investment. This all means that rising interest rates may limit returns on MLP investments.

Most of the risks to MLP investing are short-term cyclical risks, not really of much importance to a long-term investor but worrisome for someone trading in and out of the investments. Economic cycles are bound to come and go, taking interest rates and energy prices higher and lower. Long-term income investors should not worry about these risks and can be confident that MLP investments will provide strong returns over a decade or longer.

Since MLPs are already tax-advantaged, they are not appropriate investments for your 401k, IRA or other retirement accounts. Tax-exempt investors and some retirement plans may be subject to unrelated business taxable income (UBTI) on MLP investments so do not hold these investments in your retirement accounts.

The revolution in U.S. energy production is a generational phenomenon and should mean increasing or stable demand for oil & gas transportation for a very long time. The tax advantages of MLP investments should drive a respectable return, if not one that is higher than traditional stocks and bonds. Even on a conservative estimate, you should be able to earn an income return of between 3% and 5% each year from MLPs and a similar return on the investment value. A total annual return of 6% to 10% or higher is very attractive, especially when you consider that much of your income return will not be taxed until much later.

True Passive Income Potential: Income Investing

Income investing is one of the few truly passive income strategies in the book. Unlike blogging and online stores, income investing will begin to cash flow almost immediately as companies pay out their regular dividends and distributions. Unlike real estate investing, income investing takes relatively little ongoing work to maintain a stream of income.

Start-up costs to an income investing strategy are the principal drawback compared to other strategies. A cash yield of 5% is considered good for a diversified mix of dividend stocks and MLPs but would still only provide an annual income of $5,000 on a $100,000 portfolio. That is prohibitively high for some and much higher than the amount you might put down on real estate or the upfront costs to start a blog. The upside to income investing is that there are no ongoing costs other than regular deposits to your account to grow the portfolio.

The time commitment required for income investing is very low compared to other passive income strategies. You can spend hours analyzing dividend stocks and other investments but it really isn't necessary. An annual check on the business fundamentals for each investment is more than enough and some investors may not even do that.

Income momentum is strong for passive income investing because your dividends and distributions can be reinvested into the investments until income is needed to pay expenses. Do this for a couple of decades and the income you earn from prior dividends can be substantial. Besides reinvested payments, companies generally try to grow their payments as business improves which can boost your payment significantly over the years.

Continuity is also an advantage of income investing. As long as the companies you choose do not go bust or you do not sell out of the investment, you should continue to see regular payments throughout the year.

Passive Income Potential Scale

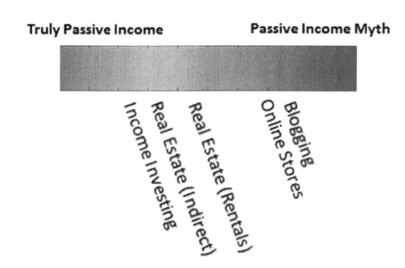

Overall, income investing is a good source of passive income and a critical part of your investment portfolio. Even if you do not need the current cash payments from an income portfolio, the regular cash yield can be reinvested to grow the portfolio and secure a stronger income in the future. While income growth may not be as high as business-related strategies like blogging or real estate, the risk and time commitment required is much lower.

Bond Investing

Besides selling stock, companies can raise money by taking out a loan. Like any other loan, an interest rate is charged on the amount and paid on a regular basis. Some loans require interest and principal to be paid off together, like the loan on your house, while others allow for only interest to be paid until a final date.

These loans are called bonds or fixed-income because of the fixed payments made until the loan matures. While a bank or brokerage firm may originate the loan, they are likely to sell it off to investors looking for a reliable income investment.

Bond investing shares similarities with income investing but goes a step further with more safety and a longer-term, hands-off approach to investing. You can invest in bonds sold by federal governments, local municipalities and more recently even the loans taken out by other people.

I have held bonds in my own portfolio for years. They provide a strong safety net against the volatility of my income that is tied to my work as an investment analyst. I began to take an interest in peer lending after the financial crisis of 2009 brought needed changes to the industry. The post-2009 market for peer loans is set to become a legitimate asset class for investors, the subject of a speech I gave recently to a conference of investment managers. Not only do peer loans provide relatively stable income but the returns are higher than you will see in traditional bonds.

Traditional Bond Investing

The traditional route to bond investing has been through government or corporate debt. Bonds are sold for a set number of years, called the bond's maturity. The company pays interest payments, usually twice a year, until the maturity of the bond when it pays the face value of the bond to investors.

Example:

- McDonald's issues $50 million in bonds with a maturity of 30 years

- The bonds have a face value (cost) of $1,000 and an interest rate of 3.5%

- McDonald's pays investors 1.75% in interest, twice a year for 30 years (3.5% total annual interest)

- At the end of 30 years, McDonald's pays the $50 million back to investors at $1,000 for each bond they hold

The basics of bond investing are straight-forward and simple. You are loaning money to a company or government for a set interest rate and a set number of years. In the event that a company cannot continue in business or make payments, bond investors are paid before stock investors. While stock investors are likely to get nothing in a bankruptcy, bond investors might get some of their money back even if it is only pennies on the dollar.

Because bondholders receive a fixed interest rate and get paid before stockholders, bonds are safer investments than stocks. They provide a stable income at lower risk but do not offer the upside return you might get in stocks. While stocks could zoom higher in any given year, your bond investments are going to pay that fixed return if you hold them to maturity.

There are details to bond trading, buying and selling frequently for a profit, just like the many trading schemes in stocks. Most investors should buy bonds to hold until they are paid off at maturity, using bonds for a stable source of passive income and a diversification from the risks in stocks.

Risks and Return to Passive Income Bond Investing

The fact that bonds are much safer than stocks makes them a great investment and they're found in the portfolios of pension funds, insurance companies and banks. All individual investors should hold a portion of their money in bonds to protect from stock market ups and downs. Those needing more stable, passive income and safety like retirees may even choose to hold the majority of their money in bonds.

Long-term corporate bonds, those issued by some of the most stable companies, have provided a 5.4% return annually over the last decade. This long-term return may change if interest rates begin to increase but rates have been dropping for more than three decades. Even if interest rates increase, bonds will continue to be a necessity in a diversified investment portfolio.

Since bonds pay a fixed interest rate and have a fixed final payment at maturity, the only thing that changes is the price someone pays for the bond. Bond prices change because the interest rate paid on other bonds and loans changes while the individual bond's rate doesn't change.

If interest rates increase then investors can earn more interest on other bonds. If someone wants to sell the old bond, they are going to have to lower the price to attract investors that have higher rate opportunities elsewhere.

On the other hand, if interest rates decrease then the bond's price will increase. This is because the fixed-rate bond is now paying a higher rate compared to what investors are getting in the market. Investors can lock-in the rate by buying the bond but they will have to offer a better price to current owners.

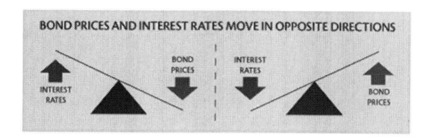

This sets up the biggest risk in bond investing. If interest rates start to increase, the value of your bonds will decrease. The beauty of being a long-term investor though is that you will still make the same return on the investment if you hold it until the bond matures. You bought the bonds and have a right to a fixed payment that doesn't change regardless of the bond's value. You will still receive the same amount when the bond matures.

The danger is only to those that choose to sell their bond investments before maturity and may be forced to sell at a lower price because of higher interest rates.

Companies issue bonds across many maturities, from short-periods less than a year to as far out as 99 years. Since rising interest rates means the bond's fixed rate is uncompetitive against newly issued bonds at higher market rates, then it stands to reason that longer-term bonds (those with longer to pay at the lower rate) are going to see their prices fall further than short-term bonds. Bonds that will mature in a couple of years will give investors the opportunity to reinvest their money in new bonds at higher rates so prices do not react quite so negatively to higher rates.

The trade-off is that longer-term bonds usually offer higher rates to start out. If a company is going to ask an investor to lock-up their money for longer, in this loan, they have to offer a higher interest rate than they would if the loan is only for a few years.

The other major risk to bonds is from inflation. Because bonds pay a fixed payment until maturity, inflation will slowly eat away at the value of that payment. Buy a 30-year bond with a $20 semi-annual payment and you'll get that same $20 twice a year for 30-years. Over three decades, that $20 is going to buy less. If inflation stays relatively low then it is not much of a problem.

The credit quality of each company is rated by firms like Moody's and Standard & Poor's. Investors look at these ratings to decide if the interest rate offered is worth the risk of loaning a lower-rated company money. The lower the rating, the higher the interest rate the company must offer to attract investors. If a company's finances deteriorate, its credit rating may get lowered. This new, higher-risk means that new investors will require a higher rate and will not pay as much for previously issued bonds. Like interest-rate risk, this downgrade-risk is not as big an issue for investors that hold their bonds to maturity because they will continue to receive the same fixed payments.

Those are the basics of bonds; interest-rate risk, downgrade-risk and the difference between short- and long-term bonds. Like stocks, there is a whole world of information and analysis within bond investing. Also as with stocks, if you plan on being a long-term investor and holding your bonds to maturity, you don't really need to worry about every facet of bond trading.

Building a Portfolio of Passive Income from Bond Investing

There is no consensus to how much of your total wealth you should have invested in bonds though nearly everyone agrees you should have some money in the asset. If you are younger, say under the age of 35, then you can probably withstand a little more risk in your portfolio and will invest more in stocks and other assets rather than bonds. Even if the stock market falls, you have at least 30 years for the value of your investments to rebound and move higher. Stocks will outperform bonds over the long-run but bonds serve a very important purpose of stability and safety.

If you are older or need income from your investments to help pay expenses, you will want a higher percentage of your investments in bonds. This goes back to the idea that, unless a company defaults, you are guaranteed to get a fixed rate of return in bonds. If the stock market happens to crash around the time you are ready to retire, a painful fact for many in 2008, the bond investor doesn't have to worry because his money is safe.

The graph below isn't meant to reflect a rule for how much of your total investments you should have invested in bonds but more of a visual aid. Notice that the young investor has very little in bonds, holding more stocks and other investments for higher returns. As the investor moves closer to retirement and protection becomes more important than seeing the portfolio value climb, more money is put to bonds. The retiree that is using his portfolio for passive income to cover living expenses has nearly all his portfolio in bonds, relatively safe and providing a constant return.

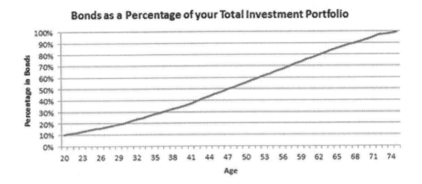

Online investing platforms like E*Trade have made it fairly easy to buy bonds. Your first decision is how much return do you need from your bond investments and at what time horizon do you want to invest. Remember, bond investing is not generally meant to make you rich but to protect the value of your portfolio. As with any investment, if you chase higher returns, you'll be forced to take more risk.

The graphic below shows current average interest rates paid for different categories of bonds at different maturities. Notice that the safest bonds, those backed by the U.S. Treasury, pay the least while bonds of lower-rated companies and local governments (municipals) pay higher rates. Bonds of longer maturity, to 30-years in the chart, pay higher rates as well.

AVERAGE YIELD BY CATEGORY   Last Updated: 06/12/2015 05 21 PM

	1Y	2Y	3Y	5Y	7Y	10Y	20Y	30Y+
CDs	.580	1.070	1.530	2.200	2.560	3.190	3.300	---
US Treasuries	.348	.795	1.151	1.768	2.123	2.348	---	2.714
US Treasury Zeroes	---	---	---	---	---	---	---	---
Agencies	.480	.771	1.384	1.953	2.560	2.999	3.747	4.152
AAA Corporates	---	.901	1.266	1.889	---	---	---	4.257
AA Corporates	.454	1.134	1.836	2.372	3.138	3.372	4.225	4.663
A Corporates	.876	1.721	2.201	2.856	3.388	3.879	4.800	5.112
AAA Municipals	.586	1.088	1.483	2.387	2.612	3.245	3.909	4.843
AA Municipals	1.365	2.454	2.412	4.221	4.386	4.714	5.120	5.482
A Municipals	1.328	2.479	3.844	4.238	4.424	4.725	6.167	5.716

Source: E*Trade

Bond ratings go all the way down to CCC- though they are only shown to A in the graphic. High-yield bonds, those from companies with weak financial positions and poor credit, are offering rates as high as 9% for 30-year terms but also offer the risk of bankruptcy before the bond matures.

One popular bond investing strategy is called "laddering" and provides a trade-off between lower rates on short-term bonds and higher interest rate risk of long-term bonds. It's a great strategy for any investor and will provide income and long-term stability.

In laddering, you invest in a group of bonds at different maturities. You might buy bonds that expire in 3, 5, 8 and 10 years. You get higher rates from your longer-term bonds but the shorter-term bonds pay off sooner. If interest rates increase, you will have your money back from the shortest-term bonds in three years and can reinvest in more bonds at the higher rate in the market. This is also a popular strategy for people that need passive income because it provides a constant stream of extra income as the near-term bonds mature and return your investment money.

Once you've decided on the characteristics of the bonds in which you want to invest, a search is made fairly easy on most online platforms. The screener below allows you to search for bonds across many different characteristics.

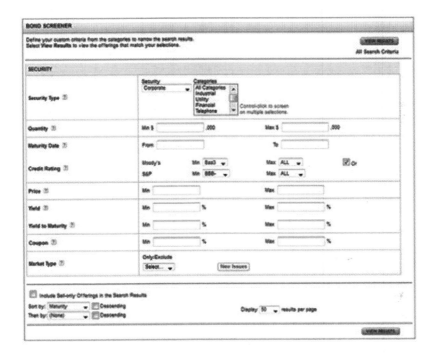

Bond ETFs as an Alternative to Bonds

Exchange Traded Funds (ETFs) are available for bond investing just like with dividend stocks, REITs and MLP investments. Investing in an ETF that itself holds a portfolio of bonds is an easy way to lower your risk by getting access to a large group of bonds all at once. Bond ETFs trade like shares of stock and usually at much lower prices than individual bonds.

The fact that bond ETFs do not mature means there is no yield-to-maturity for the fund. You really don't know what kind of return you will get because it all depends on when you sell the fund, not when it matures. The bonds in the portfolio lose value when interest rates increase so the shares of the ETF also decrease in price with rising rates. This means you could be left with a lower return if you have to sell shares at a time when rates are increasing.

There are fewer bond ETFs than those that invest in stocks. It is fairly easy to put together a diversified portfolio of bonds with just a few ETFs. Two of my favorite bond ETFs are:

The iShares Core US Aggregate Bond (NYSE: AGG) pays a dividend yield of 2.28% and charges a super-low 0.09% expense ratio. Bonds issued by the U.S. Treasury make up 38% of the fund and another 30% of the fund is invested in bonds like Fannie Mae with the banking of the government. Since the bonds are very safe, the return is not going to be as high but will be more stable. The fund has provided investors with a 4.77% annual return over the last ten years.

The SPDR Barclays High Yield Bond (NYSE: JNK) pays a dividend yield of 5.77% and charges a 0.4% expense ratio. The fund holds 802 bonds that mature in an average of 6.4 years. The time to maturity is important because an increase in interest rates affects short-maturity bonds less than it does longer-dated bonds. This means the bonds in the fund should not decrease in value quite as quickly as the prices in the longer-dated Aggregate Bond fund.

Another reason to hold shares in the high-yield fund is because of the way the bonds react to the economy and interest rates. An increase in rates will still decrease the price of high-yield bonds but not as much as with other bonds because high-yield bonds follow the economy more closely. Since the companies that issue high-yield bonds are riskier than other companies, uncertainty over the companies' ability to repay debt is higher. A growing economy, usually happening the same time interest rates are increasing, means these companies have a better chance at paying debt. That lower risk to payment usually helps high-yield bond prices not fall as much as other bonds.

There are hundreds of other bond ETFs to buy but you really don't need too many for a diversified portfolio. You might consider adding a fund with foreign bonds as well but that would be the extent you would need.

Peer Lending

Peer lending hit a snag in 2008 along with the rest of the loan market but has rebounded and is now a $10 billion+ market. The revolution in funding has opened up a whole new world to borrowers and investors alike. New computer programs for measuring loan risk mean a safer investment that will withstand the next drop in the business cycle and could offer investors an opportunity to diversify their risk in stocks.

Peer lending is quickly emerging as a new asset class and one of the strongest forms of passive income for investors.

What is Peer Lending?

The concept of peer lending couldn't be simpler and there is really very little difference with the traditional bank loan process. Peer lending is the evolution of bank loans into the online and social revolution.

A borrower fills out an application for an unsecured personal loan of up to $35,000 on one of the online lending sites which verify employment and other information. The application is posted to the website where investors choose if they want to invest in a portion of the loan, from as little as $25 each. If the loan is fully funded, the money is released to the borrower's bank account and monthly payments are made directly to the website. The website handles collection and processing while passing payments through to the investors.

Investing in bank loans is nothing new, investors have been buying loan portfolios for ages. Traditionally, banks would issue loans and then either sell those loans to an investment firm or bundle the loans themselves. Bundling is the process of grouping loans together by characteristics like loan maturity or borrower risk. Bundling loans, a process called securitization, serves two purposes:

- It spreads the risk out across many loans. Investors do not have to worry as much about a particular loan defaulting because there are many loans in the portfolio

- It helps investors match their needs better by offering them a group of loans that will pay off over the preferred time and offers a preferred risk-return tradeoff

The bank or investment firm then sells the bundled loans to investors that are looking for higher returns than corporate bonds but relative safety compared to stocks. Of course, the bank and investment firm both take their cut of the returns for costs and profit.

Peer lending effectively removes the middleman and matches borrowers and investors directly. The peer lending platforms charge a fee of around 5% to borrowers for origination and loan servicing. Beyond this fee, all borrower payments are passed through to investors. Because peer lending platforms do not need a physical bank branch, it is much cheaper to originate loans and cost savings can be passed down to investors.

After a peer loan application is reviewed, including a check on the borrower's credit report, the loan is assigned a risk category and an interest rate according to several factors. Loans are normally made for periods of between three and five years.

1. Create your loan listing
2. Investors commit funds to your loan
3. Receive your money!
4. Make monthly payments

Rates for peer loans are competitive with personal loans from traditional banks. Borrowers with very good credit can currently get an APR as low as 6.0% while the average rate is 13% across all loans. In the past, most loans (80%) have been for debt consolidation, paying off high-interest credit cards, but the market is opening up quickly to other types of loans including small business and student loans.

Why invest in Peer Loans?

With the low rates offered on traditional bond investments, and the likelihood that low rates will continue for quite some time, the higher returns on peer loans have been attracting a lot of attention. Treasury bonds are paying less than 1% after inflation and even riskier corporate bonds only offer a yield of a few percent.

Peer loans originated on the Prosper website over the four years to October 2014 returned an annualized 9.0%, and that was after removing losses on defaulted loans. Average interest rates of 7.2% on the safest credit rating offered a 5.5% return after defaults. That is comparable to the return on the lowest-rated corporate bonds but these loans are made to borrowers with exceptional credit.

Prosper Loan Returns November 2005- October 2014

Rating	# Loans	$Amount Loans	Actual Effective Yield	Actual Loss Rate	Actual Return	Average Credit Score
AA	3,406	$36,386,483	7.2%	1.8%	5.5%	798
A	8,670	$90,684,178	10.0%	3.5%	6.5%	758
B	9,069	$93,578,107	14.2%	5.0%	9.3%	729
C	9,737	$87,934,359	18.2%	7.4%	10.8%	711
D	10,953	$73,091,021	22.0%	11.5%	10.5%	696
E	7,057	$29,295,576	25.8%	15.1%	10.6%	676
HR	6,284	$21,606,091	27.0%	16.6%	10.4%	691
All	**55,176**	**$432,575,816**	**16.3%**	**7.3%**	**9.0%**	**726**

Source: Prosper Site Statistics

Peer loans are emerging as a new asset class for investors with characteristics different from stocks, bonds and real estate. Because they are debt obligations with fixed terms, peer loans offer more certainty than stocks. As long as the loan is paid off, you know what kind of return you will get over the life of the investment.

Because personal lines of credit carry more risk than corporate loans, the investments offer a higher return than traditional bonds. The shorter period on loans means they are not affected as much by interest rate changes. Most loans are made to borrowers with credit scores of 700 or above with the safest categories experiencing very low default rates.

Beyond strong returns, peer loans offer diversification from a stock and bond portfolio. Using the S&P Experian Consumer Credit Index as a proxy for peer loans, we find almost no correlation (0.014) with stocks over the last five years and a very low (0.28) correlation with bonds. This means that not only can investors see higher returns on peer loans but, combined with a portfolio of stocks and bonds, you can reduce your risk significantly.

How to Create a Passive Income from Peer Loan Investing

The two largest peer lending platforms, Lending Club and Prosper Marketplace, make it extremely easy to manage a peer lending portfolio.

Opening an investor account on Prosper takes about five minutes requiring your contact and bank account information. If you are outside one of the 32 states that allow investment in peer lending, you may have to open up a Folio Investing account to get access but the returns will be the same. Funds can be transferred directly from your bank account and payments are made by direct deposit.

Once you've funded your investment account, it is time to look at different loans on the site. Borrowers are ranked on a scale between AA to HR according to their credit history and other loan details. You can also search for loans that fit certain criteria and may have a lower chance at default.

Source: Prosper Marketplace

There are upwards of 40 criteria that you can select or change to find the loans in which you want to invest. Most criteria do not really matter much when it comes to return on the portfolio but there are some that have helped to lower risk and increase return.

I like to invest in borrowers with no credit inquiries in the last six months and with a debt-to-income of less than 25 percent. The fact that the borrower has no credit inquiries means they have not been scrambling to open new credit accounts and borrow money. Having a lower debt-to-income ratio means they are not getting over their head with debt. Selecting higher-risk loans with these two criteria usually means borrowers that will pay higher rates but are not necessarily in financial trouble.

Looking through loan listings, you can invest from $25 and up in loans that meet your criteria. The borrower pays all fees so investing doesn't cost anything. Once the loan is fully funded by investors, the borrower gets their money and you should start seeing payments show up in your account in less than two months.

Prosper offers a Quick Invest feature where you set your loan criteria and the platform will automatically select those loans that meet the requirements. You decide how much to invest in each and then approve an investment in the entire portfolio all at once. It takes some of the fun out of looking at each individual loan, basically becoming a loan officer, but can make the process easier and much faster.

Since loans gradually pay off over three to five years, you will want to set regular times to reinvest your money. The payments on loans are a nice return but you will earn nothing on the interest until you reinvest it into another loan. There is not yet much of a secondary market for peer loans, buying and selling existing loans, so be ready to have the money locked-up until the loan pays off. This is a good thing for most investors as it prevents them from panic-selling.

If you are investing for income to pay living expenses, you would just withdraw the interest paid on your peer loans each month instead of reinvesting it into more loans.

Risks and Return on Peer Loan Investing

Like any investment strategy, there are risks to peer lending. Most of the risks come from investors reaching too far for higher returns and not understanding concepts like diversification. Let's look at the two major risks in peer loan investing before moving on to returns you can expect.

The backbone of any investment strategy is your need for return balanced by your personal tolerance for risk. How many investors have jumped into a hot penny stock on the hope of getting rich quick only to lose money after the stock crumbles? There is good money to be made in stocks of small companies but the risk is more than many can stomach.

The same is true for peer lending investors. Too many investors see double-digit rates as high as 30% on loans and put all their money into the high-risk category. Their sense of euphoria and hopes for an early retirement soon turn to anguish when loans start to default. While loans in the HR category on Prosper have earned a solid 10% annually, nearly 17% of them have defaulted. Investors not ready for that level of risk sour quickly on peer lending when loans start to default. They avoid looking at their account and close it out once their loans mature.

I'm going to tell you THE secret to success in investing...ready? You don't need super high rates of return. Over 25 years at an annual rate of just 7.5%, your portfolio will grow to $285,507 with contributions of just $350 each month. That's a gain of more than $180,000, over the period and on a relatively modest rate of return and very little contributed.

The problem is that people rush into high-risk investments and end up losing their shirt. They never see that 7.5% annual return and they never see what their life could be like meeting their financial goals.

If you have a few decades before you need a stable income and can handle higher risk, then invest in higher-risk categories of peer loans. If you need more safety and less volatility, then invest only in the safer categories.

Diversification is another key risk, but also an opportunity in peer loan investing. Diversification is the idea that, if you spread your investments out over different places then some will go up even when others are going down. For many investors, this means buying stocks and bonds since the two rarely fall or rise at the same time.

The chart, provided by Lending Club, shows the difference in portfolio returns by how many loans are held.

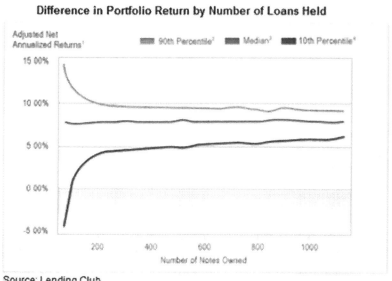

Difference in Portfolio Return by Number of Loans Held

You can see from the graph that if your portfolio holds less than 100 loans, you are setting yourself up for very good or very bad returns. While you may be able to achieve stellar returns over a couple of years, the chances are likely that your luck will run out eventually. Your portfolio is exposed to the chance that a few defaulting loans will send overall returns tumbling. The chart also shows that very little additional diversification is gained by holding more than 200 individual loans.

Beyond the number of loans in which you invest, it is also a good idea to spread your investment out over at least a few loan-risk categories as well. This will give you the benefit of higher rates in some categories and the stability of payments in others.

I recommend a portfolio of between 125 and 175 loans to give yourself enough diversification without loosing the opportunity to make higher returns on a good loan-selection strategy. Most of your loans can be bought using the website's automated investing tool which helps pick loans according to your pre-set criteria. Setting a portion of your investing on auto-pilot also helps reduce the time you spend and make it a more passive income strategy. You might try manually selecting between 25 and 50 loans to improve your chances of higher returns through good criteria like debt-to-income and credit inquiries.

Since peer loans like personal bonds, they carry the same type of interest rate risk as do corporate bonds. Two factors make interest rates less of an issue for peer loans than for bonds.

- Since peer loans are for shorter periods, usually three to five years, changing interest rates do not affect the price much.

- Since peer loans are not traded as much, you normally buy and hold your loans until they are paid off. Prices of older loans do not have to adjust to attract new buyers as rates increase or decrease.

Returns on a peer loan portfolio can be quite good and help to boost your overall portfolio returns. I invest in the middle three categories on Prosper (B, C and D) for a good mix of risk and return. Returns differ a little from year to year but hover around 10% on the investment. Even on a relatively safe portfolio invested in the safest two categories you can expect returns between 5% and 7% a year.

Passive Income Potential: Bond and Loan Investing

Bond investing provides one of the most passive streams of income you can find. The market for bonds is very large and prices reflect the trade-off between rates, credit quality and bond maturity. You select bonds at a credit rating with which you feel comfortable and a rate and term that you need.

Since bonds are best held to maturity for most investors, guaranteeing the return available when you bought the bond, there is less to worry about than with stocks. While many investors spend countless hours analyzing and deciding whether to sell their stock investments, bonds are a real buy-and-hold investment because they have a fixed return and a fixed lifespan.

Start-up costs are the one drawback to bonds because individual bonds are generally more expensive than individual shares of stock and financing is not usually offered. Most bonds have a face value, the amount you will get back when it matures, of $1,000 each. There are circumstances where you will pay less than this but you are still looking at several hundred dollars for each bond you buy. This makes it difficult for new investors to start out with a diversified portfolio of bonds from different companies and different maturities.

The time commitment for investing in bonds is next to nothing. You select the bonds in which you want to invest given how long you want to invest and the credit quality you want. Once you buy a bond, you're return is locked-in unless the company files bankruptcy or you sell the bond. This makes bonds a real set-it and forget-it investment.

Income momentum is respectable for bond investing though not as good as with income investing or indirect real estate investing. You can reinvest your bond payments into more bonds for faster income growth but the lower rate of return means that growth is not likely to be very fast. Bonds are not meant as the get-rich-quick investment but more the protect-my-future investment.

Continuity of income is another upside for bonds since you are assured of getting your fixed payments and the maturity payment at the end of the term. Invest in high enough quality bonds and the risk of default is next to zero. Even if the company defaults, you may receive some money back while stock investors will get nothing.

Passive Income Potential Scale

Truly Passive Income   **Passive Income Myth**

Bond and Loan Investing
Income Investing
Real Estate (Indirect)
Real Estate (Rentals)
Online Stores
Blogging

Choosing your Passive Income Path

The three most passive income strategies; bonds, income investing and indirect real estate investing should be a part of everyone's diversified portfolio of investments. Holding a mix of bonds, dividend stocks, MLPs and REITs along with common stocks will help lower risk in your overall portfolio and smooth returns. The minimum you hold in each of these will vary with your age and risk tolerance but you might consider holding between 5% and 15% in each strategy.

Whether you choose to invest more heavily in one of these strategies or to explore income in the other passive income strategies will be up to you. After having read this book, I hope you have a better idea of the work involved to be successful within each.

Even within the investments that should be in your basic investing portfolio, you may decide to devote extra time and more of your money into the strategy. While I have suggested a simple buy-and-hold process for bonds and dividend stocks, your passion for the strategies may lead you to delve deeper into the analysis and do more trading.

You may decide that you will avoid direct real estate investments, peer loans, and online assets altogether. Real estate rentals and online assets require much more work than many are willing to commit. While income potential and returns may be very good, the work involved just isn't for everyone.

If you do have the passion and time to participate in some of the more intensive passive income strategies, there is good long-term potential in income and profits. After a while, you may find that you're making enough money to outsource management and can convert the investment to truly passive income.

After having managed my own real estate rentals to the point where cash flow after expenses and mortgage payments is sufficient to cover management as well, I have outsourced a lot of the work in favor of spending more time developing my two blogs. I also hold the majority of my investment portfolio in the three passive income ideas listed; dividend stocks, REITs and MLPs. Someday I hope to have developed the blogs enough to outsource some of the management there as well, creating a passive income stream from nearly every strategy discussed.

As with most myths, there is some fact and some fiction within passive income strategies. There is also a lesson to be learned that can save you from falling for all the get-rich-schemes out there. Notice that the most passive of the strategies, those that truly can be set-and-forget with little time commitment, offer the lowest returns.

Bonds offer a nearly guaranteed return and a very passive approach but the annual yield for most investments will be below five percent. Contrast that with the work involved and potential in blogging and online stores. There are bloggers that make five-figure paychecks a month and sell their blogs for hundreds of thousands, but these are by far the exception rather than the rule. Building a profitable blog or online store takes years of work and there's still the risk that it will never yield a high return.

Higher profits almost always require more work and higher risk. If it were not the case, everyone would be taking advantage of the strategy and retiring early to paradise. Anyone trying to pitch you on the ease of a huge source of passive income is probably trying to sell you their strategy for a fee, or worse yet, get you hooked into a scam.

This isn't meant to scare you from any particular strategy, only to inform you and empower you to make a wiser decision. Knowing what is required to be successful will mean you're better prepared to stick it out and eventually be successful, rather than quitting disappointed before your payday comes.

A Special Request

I hope you've enjoyed The Passive Income Myth and found the advice to be helpful in planning your income investments. Throughout the book, I've tried to emphasize the benefit to a simple and basic strategy that meets YOUR financial goals. There's no lack of ways to complicate your investing strategy but the simplest approach will get you to where you want to be with the least amount of headache and sleepless nights.

I'd like to ask one favor as you finish reading the book. Reader reviews are extremely important to the success of a book on Amazon. Reviews play a big part in determining the rank of a book and how many people see it when searching.

If you found the book to be helpful, would you please leave a review on the Amazon page?

It's really easy to do and does not have to be a long, detailed review.

Please click here to leave a review on Amazon

- Just go to the book's page on Amazon (or through the link above) and click on "customer reviews" or scroll down and click on "Write a customer review"

- Your review can be as short as a sentence or as long as you like. Just try describing what you liked about the book and any particular points from a chapter.

I always appreciate honest reviews. Thank you so much!

Resources

Below are links to informational resources within each passive income strategy. I have removed links within the content of the book to make it less distracting but thought a resource page would be helpful. Use the links below to get more information on the specific strategy or sector. Be aware that many of these sites, as a part of their industry, may be biased to the upside potential within the industry. You should expect the National Association of Real Estate Investment Trusts (NAREIT) to be enthusiastic about prospects for real estate and REITs. Study the information available but use your own judgment is analyzing the strategies.

Round out your investing plan with the best investments in dividends, emerging markets, stocks and bonds. Check out the Step-by-Step Investing series of books. Each book is a quick read on a specific investing topic, showing you how to customize a strategy that meets your needs.

Learn the secret to building an investing strategy that will meet YOUR needs. The first book in the series covers 10 basic rules of investing you must remember to avoid losing money. You'll get the secret to winning the stock market game as well as a step-by-step strategy for buying stocks. ***Click here to buy Step-by-Step Investing.***

Learn how to put dividend stocks in your portfolio and money in your pocket! This book covers income investments like REITs, MLPs and dividend stocks that have provided strong returns and a regular cash return. ***Click here to buy Step-by-Step Dividend Investing.***

Learn the secret to bond investing and how to balance your investments with safety. This book covers how to buy bonds and a simple strategy that will provide a stable income stream you can live on. ***Click here to buy Step-by-Step Bond Investing.***

Learn how to add growth to your investments through stocks from the fastest growing countries in the world. This book shows you how to boost returns and lower risk by diversifying in emerging markets. ***Click here to buy Step-by-Step Emerging Market Investing.***

Real Estate

National Association of Real Estate Investment Trusts (NAREIT) – Information, news and research on REITs and Real Estate

Realtor.com – National organization of realtors and provides MLS listings

National Tax Lien Association – News and advocacy for tax lien industry

Zillow – Residential real estate portal that lists MLS and other for sale listings

FHA Loans website – official HUD.gov site

Fannie Mae Homepath – Fannie Mae REO homes for sale and loans

Blogging & Online Stores

Google Adsense Academy – A detailed guide by Google to help you get the most of your Adsense advertising

Wordpress – The structure for your blog where you will build it out. Make sure you pay for your own site and not use the free solution.

Google Analytics – You'll need this to keep track of traffic on your blog and from where visitors are coming.

Google Webmaster Tools – You'll need this to help develop the SEO on your blog and track information.

Upwork – formerly oDesk, a place to find outsourced work to help with your blog. Be warned that hiring the cheapest bidder will often lead to disappointment and poor service.

Shopify – online store and blogging platform

Flexoffers – affiliate advertising network

Income Investing

National Association of Publicly Traded Partnerships (NAPTP) – trade organization for MLP investments with news and information

Investopedia Dividend University – introduction to dividends

Bonds

Investopedia Bond University – introduction to bonds

Bloomberg Rates – interest rates on government and corporate bonds as well as news and analysis

Prosper – peer lending platform with investing overview and data on loans

Lending Club – peer lending platform with investing overview and data on loans

NSR Platform – informational site on peer loan investing with data for both Prosper and Lending Club. Includes an interesting screener to help select your loan investing criteria.

Made in the USA
Lexington, KY
07 May 2018